Giants Etched Across the Land and Sea

Spoils of War That Made the Earth

by Jennifer Lind

Table of Contents

Preface

The past has been hidden from you! But, what does the future entail? Not only did antediluvian Giants once roam the Earth, but Giants have been on this planet every time the Earth has gone through an upheaval that led to a world-wide cataclysm—whether the cataclysm was natural or man-made. Every time around this upheaval occurs, the surviving beings on this planet become smaller and smaller over the hundreds of thousands—if not millions—of years.

The rocks and dirt of the Earth are remnants of Giants—plain and simple. All of it. Up to and including Tia maat Herself. Check it out, folks! There is a new antagonist in town to call whack-a-doodle: if you'd all point your crosshairs in this direction...

The truth is, the Earth is older than either side of the "flat Earth" debate thinks. First of all, the Earth is a lot bigger than we've been told. Yes, the Earth is flat but only sometimes—sometimes, She is round. You see, the Earth evolves its form like a human being goes through their phases of development, as if from birth to ascension.

Mostly, the Earth's voluptuous shape takes on valleys and peaks as She turns, folds within them, and unfolds without. For you see, Her shape is that of a Torus: ever changing, taking shapes constant from disc to circle to sphere and back again.

Lately, She is rotund from the displaced water inside of Her. Let's send a collective burst of positive thought/e-motion vibrations Her way to alleviate the excess fluid from her legs, stomach, and eyes...

The Earth is not stationary—not by any means, She moves along in tandem with the other celestial bodies in our solar system by spiraling around the central sun. I believe that She changes according to the perception and vantage point of the observer, like all other subatomic particles that coalesce and form into matter.

Human beings have a smaller function within this larger organism in which we live—I'm an *anti*-subatomic particle, observe me and I stand still!

Don't be a rebel without a clue—go rogue and become a virulent spore. There is a *firmament*, of course—we are quarantined and hermetically sealed under it...for every one else's protection. The ice wall is real, also—we are too curious for our own good, giving the bad guys all our good ideas for them to exploit and corrupt the rest of us. *The Truman Show* is very real in many ways.

Things are not always what they seem, and nothing's what it looks like. Many, if not most (whether they realize it or not) are ready for the truth.

So, now all you crackpots can call this coo coo, crazy. Go ahead, be the pot! It's better than being a tool.

Don't be a tool!

Bring it.

You've all been served

~Peace~

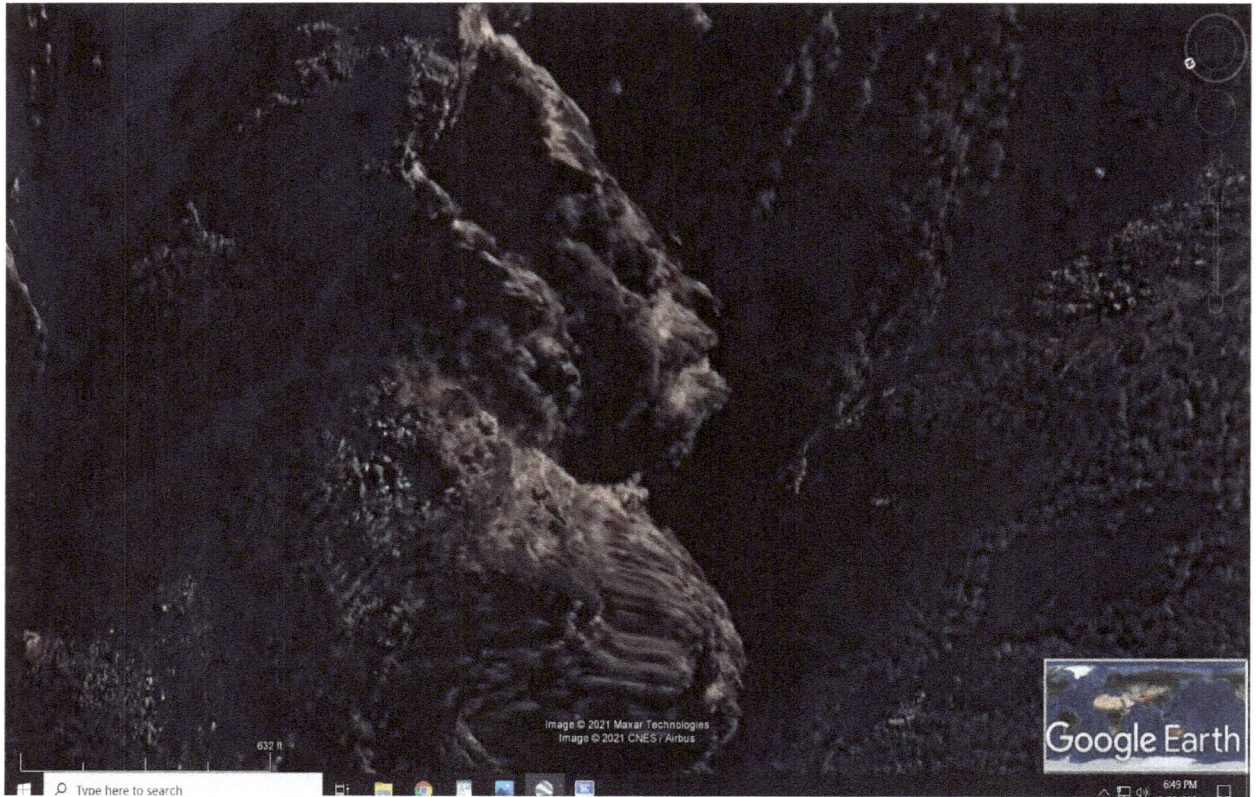

Figure 1. (Google, 2021) Perfect profile in the Himalayas.

I shall arrive like the Promise of Spring

And, in the ensuing Insanity of Fighting for Peace lies the insignificant significant, the Unlucky Lucky, the simply complicated divided by a negative: one tested, tried, and true Free Agent—there are many odds against me but also much determination on my part to work through the dismissive apathy of others.

This one word is for all disablers, naysayers, waylayers, and invalidators:

Ahimsa

Chapter 0: *Ouroboros of Ophiuchus: Wrangling the Closed Logos of Life, Death, Reincarnation

Prelude to a Dream

This is a work in progress—I intend to add to or slightly rework the information as it reveals itself. So, these chapters are still unfolding and there will be more to present!

This work is presented with the assumption that Giants did in fact, exist. Not once or twice or even three times; with every turn of the tide, with each age comes the Giant—just smaller and smaller in scale.

This book is also written with the assumption that this planet is far larger than we've all been taught. Far, far larger. To end the argument before it even begins, we will assume that the planet is neither round *nor* flat but each at different turns from Her varied toroid shape.

Much of the time, She more resembles a Klein Bottle more than a sphere: a torus rather than a disk.

For this book, I have decided to structure these essays as intellectual "shorts" to allow for the natural flow of information without force or without any more self-will than is necessary to see the task through to its writing and publication. *Much of this text appears as commentary which may be only marginally related to the topic;* in reality, this free-flowing approach to education is what allows the lessons of this text on Giants to shine through!

I have grappled with the idea of writing about Giants for a long time. That I have not the accomplished level of "education" that might've instantly qualified (or outcast me for) any of what I am suggesting here, does not work in my favor. However, having that "education" perhaps would have blinded me from seeing these things as they are, assuming they are what I'm suggesting...

I understand that what I am stating in this book may strike you as unfounded or foolish, and that I "must be uneducated about how geology works" and I "clearly have pareidolia," and so on. I realize how whack this is going to sound to most people having been taught all that we have, since we were in the indoctrination centers known as schools. More on that later...

It shouldn't matter how much education one needs to have to point out the obvious from one human being to another. Period! If I were to see a spaceship—a UFO—suddenly, I am not going to run to the nearest PhD in rocket science for confirmation that that's what I saw—right? I would just know!

Okay, perhaps that's not the greatest argument...

But, the bottom line is there is still the conveyance of the truth from one human being to another in what appears to be obvious in the very photographs of the Earth Herself. Were it not for all the ancient text that is very pointed about the descriptions of Giants or about the war(s) between "gods and men," "Titans," or "angels and demons," I might have been dismissive of what I'm seeing on Google Earth. Instead—it's made me have a much closer look at it...

To me, it's very clear what has happened, in a general sense, because Giants are all over the landscape and because the bodies of giants *are* the landscape; they are under the water, in and under the ice. Giants are petrified, burned, melted, or flashed onto the landscape and in many places can still easily be seen.

Earth even cleverly reveals Her past in the clouds—while that may seem like a stretch of the imagination, the more I see, the more I understand. The more anomalies I see in clouds and weather pattern formations—the more I am convinced that just as water holds memory and would in cloud formation (as clouds are water), so does the air hold memory (which is sometimes seen as ghosts).

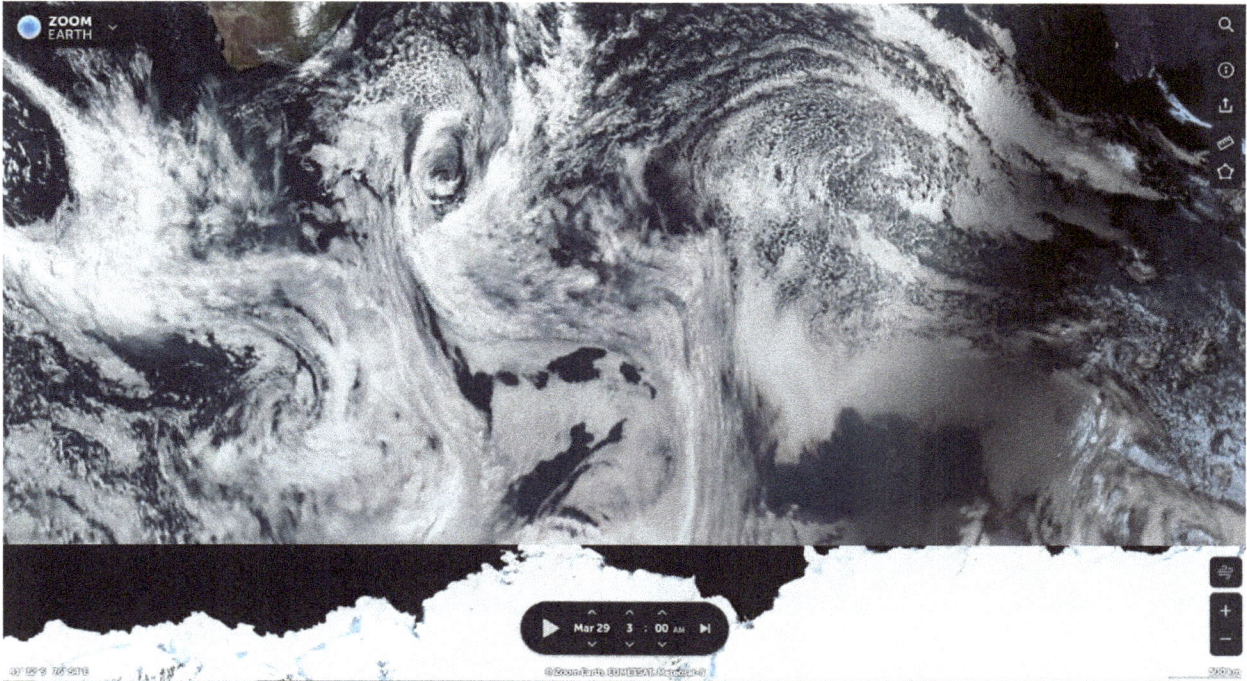

Figure 2. (Zoom Earth, n.d.) This one leaves little doubt as the face is easily seen over a huge area of the earth.

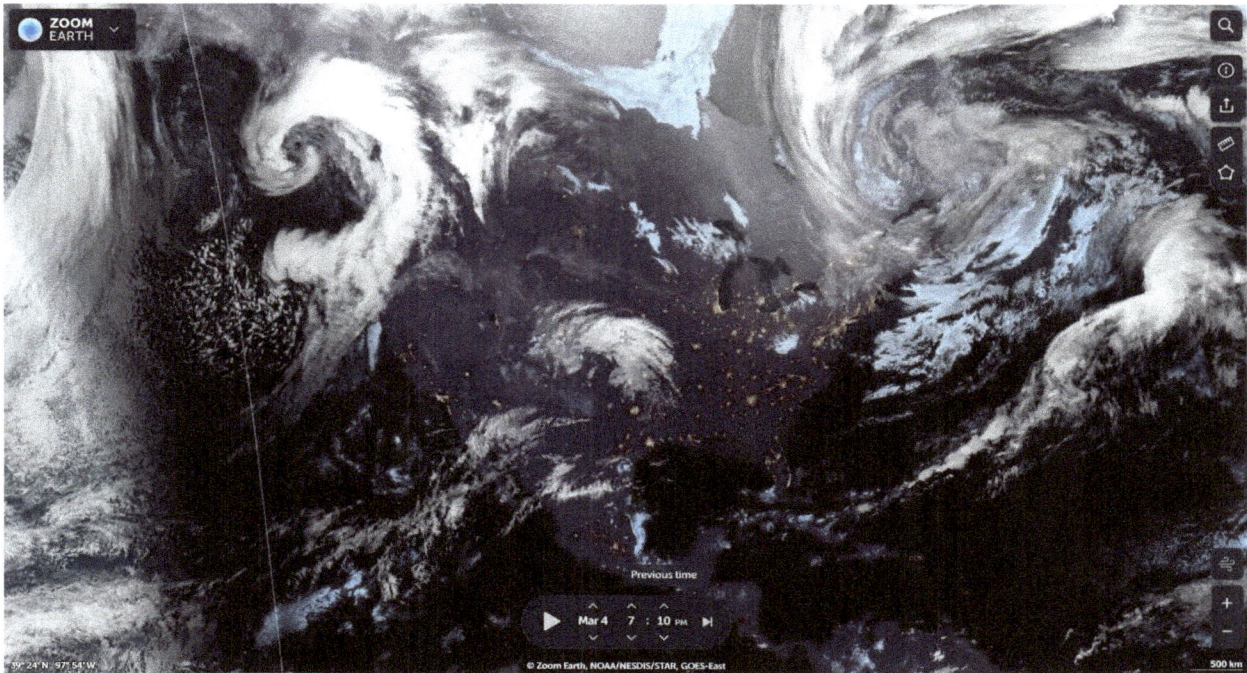

Figure 3. (Zoom, n.d.) Head and even a hand.

Figure 4. (Google, 2014, December 13) Grimacing cloud.

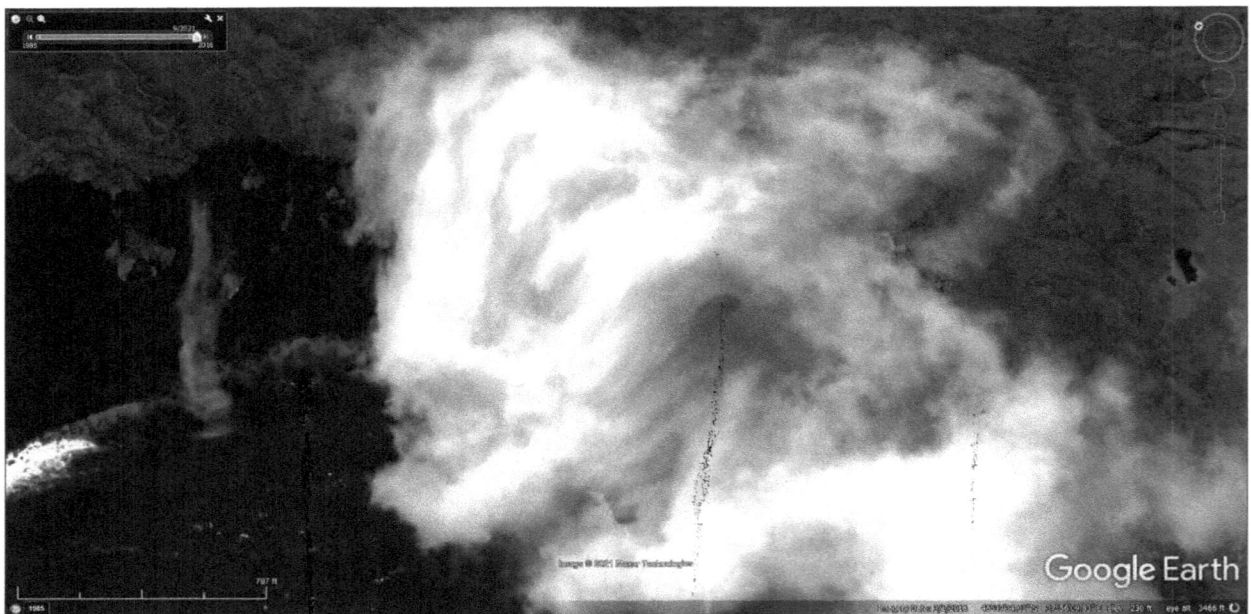

Figure 5. (Google, 2016, March 1). This figure seems to have hands pulling at the head.

I ask: how can one look at any of these clouds and convince themselves that this is only their imagination? How is anyone going to tell you that you have pareidolia—that it's all in your head? Why would these clouds appear like this if it didn't reflect the reality of the past at some point in time?

The clouds portray astral remnants of past actions which were executed by such massive beings that a swipe of their hand in your direction (if you are much smaller—like our present size) would cause a great gust of wind, and you would be knocked off your feet—if not swept up and dashed back down to the ground, dead!

Human beings have been the target of psychological operations from "experts" and those in academia (and those brainwashed by academia), most notably by the use of gaslighting to discredit rogue thinkers. It's the oldest mind game in the book—we will never know how often these operations have worked and the pile of dead researchers, scientists etc. that resulted.

But, what those same brainwashed people don't realize is that when academia is stripped of all its pretenses, all of its misleading and misled conclusions—leaving no room for alternative insight—that pigeonhole and condemn others for not blindly following their academic rigid orthodoxy and dogma, what is left? Is that who we are trying to take our cues from, emulate, model after, and look up to—after all?

After everything that people have endured and suffered at the hands of "experts" (who have the degrees that say they are the best at what they have been educated to do). Forever practicing! They can't perfect something they know they can't master. They may as well call what scientists do, too, like doctors and lawyers, a "practice"—a hopelessly flawed and incomplete diagnosis, prognosis, closing argument, hypothesis and theory forever falling short of truly remedying the situation. Nobody is getting healed...

Has anyone ever seen the doctor to be healed of their malady? No—because actually healing the sick does not produce repeat paying patients. The fact that most of the medical establishment is comfortable with the pharmaceutical companies cranking out synthetics instead of sticking with natural based solutions and drugs is reprehensible. And even more distressing is all because no one can patent natural ingredients but anyone can patent a synthetic to be adulterated and made to be more toxic than the original malady would be deadly to the patient, is amoral.

The same thing is exactly true when it comes to religion: anywhere where the few have control (in some way) over the many and use fear and intimidation and manipulation tactics to get you to comply with their demands...that sounds familiar! It seems that these days it's the media and the Internet doing these very things.

And, because of this, few have the courage or the audacity to challenge the narrative of academia, religion, or the media. Nobody wants to have their careers and reputations ruined by standing up to so-called scholars. So-called experts in their fields. For example, real journalists' primary ethic is to pursue the Truth no matter what, no matter what their peers tell them, no matter what the political climate as long as you just read this script and do and say as directed.

The polarization of Americans is largely pumped up by the media. The only people fighting are the ones that have violently defended their stance—in no matter what capacity—and they are being orchestrated like puppets towards a particular end; they can't see past their own hate and intolerance of others to comprehend what pawns they are themselves in someone else's scheme. In my lifetime, the roles of those calling themselves liberals has flipped a 180, what started out as peaceful, "live and let live" has now become intolerant, judgmental, clannish and closed to mature and open dialogue.

It's the same with the flag-wavers who would send their own kids off to war to fight for a country whose government has such little regard for their lives. And it's not even as though this country (or any country) is right in their war waging—not in the least!

It's a clear and conscious decision on the part of the powers that be to infiltrate and implement toxic democracy in every country and government. In doing this, we use up every resource, gather up every artifact, destroy any ancient histories. Why do you think they are bombing everywhere in the Middle East? To destroy ancient history so they(American cabal) can continue to falsify and fabricate the history at any point. To use a recent example, did you know that over 17,000 artifacts were stolen from Iraq after the 2003 U.S. invasion, and some of these artifacts were destroyed? (Arraf, 2021). What if one of the goals of the invasion was to recover this stolen history? This is not a conspiracy theory—the Guardian and Reuters write about it!

It's all the same thing. Whether it's WW1, WW2, the Korean War, Vietnam, the Persian Gulf, or Afghanistan—neutralize and vaporize "the enemy" and their history from the face of the earth. *There is no enemy and there never was.* America created the conflicts, in pursuit of the all-mighty dollar with capitalism and power through world domination. Let's face it, America is the big bully of the world.

Even the "lingo" that is used by the powers that be to obfuscate the truth reeks of hypocrisy, nepotism, and unaccountability which is assumed to be above reproach (because of an extensive and lengthy brainwashing—uh, I mean education!) And then you, perhaps, get a "reputable" place in society's eyes if you submit to this indoctrination that you don't even realize you are submitting to.

But, it's time we all wake up and yearn to eat the sweet manna of truth that has been kept from the masses. The knowledge that Giants were/are real is about as close to the "ground" as a foundation slab as we can actually grasp a hold of to build a structure that is contingent upon the various Truths that are missing from the *correct* and *objective* narrative that leaves space and material to build a solid structure upon.

Let me say right here that I am not trying to oppose any one person or any group of people but rather challenging a *construct of ideas* that we have been conditioned and miseducated by since the dawn of civilization, certainly since the creation of money.

A construct that has long taken on a life of its own and has been carefully and methodically planned and carried out as sure as the real history of this "New Atlantis" has been omitted from the history books taught to us in school.

The whole system was set up to fail, so that the few can benefit from the many. They are actively planning the demise of most of us. If you can't or won't see this, then their plan is certainly working and you will be an unwitting(by refusal of denial) cause of easement for their plan to work the way they want. Do you think and honestly believe they would spare you oh forever piously patriotic one? Your loyalty is wasted soldier, you have been duped. This is 2023 and I'm sure your early messages were ones built around the trauma of 911 and the drama of who our corrupt government was to wrongly and falsely blame. The whole thing reeks inside job. The official narrative of it is just like a lot of glibly explained half-truths and complete misconceptions, contradictions and inconsistencies.

Ya wanna keep the peace amongst the people and keep them placated? After all our lives being told this is the greatest nation on the face of the planet..Divert the attention. Snap on the football game and let the alcohol flow. Have an awards show. Make some silly celebrity gossip the hot topic of debate-Fox "entertainment news" will be happy to distract you with utter tripe while the real news gets but a glance. Or create a scenario whereby you come out a "hero". Point the finger at the faction you want to manipulate and take-over by forcing the central banking system onto its government like they did in Afghanistan. And that was merely one excuse to invade.

So of course if you want to keep the suspicious eyes off you, you blame someone else! Especially one who's not playing by the rules in any other arena. It's childish and so transparent and of course the media is central to this agenda because dumb people believe the news without one thought as to why we all are told what we are told. Because it's a fact that people are easy to confound, easy to be told what to do and how to think and what to think about. It's being done just like that and hardly anyone who's truly awake can convince those who are sleep walking, for that would disrupt people's little pink clouds. It's easier to go with the grain, not step out of line and just shut up and do as you are told, plus it's socially acceptable—no socially mandatory to fall in line.

People don't want to have to think for themselves and carve out their own path, their own way. Doing that would make them a target for others to foist their own insecurities, weaknesses and shortcomings onto. Hell the government has normalized the delusion of democracy, psychopathic capitalist goals and the idea of ownership; the media has normalized lying, politics and the us-versus-them, two-party majority; society embraces narcissism and "bling". So obviously the masses have normalized senseless violence and in-your-face hypersexuality with diminished sensitivity to these same things with nothing left to one's imagination but for how to play out the most vilest of scenarios just because there is "nothing new under the sun".

So what's happening is history repeating itself through reliving the original trauma when we were present and alive during civilizations past being upended through war, natural cataclysm or some otherwise mass trauma.

The masses always seem to get the watered down, diluted and delusive versions of the convoluted truth, or we get a pack of lies wrapped around a kernel of truth. It's easier to target a person or people than it is to target an idea. We seem to want to hold *someone* accountable-doesn't matter in the end who, just like on the other side of that same coin people want someone to swoop in and play the part of savior.

We've all normalized dysfunction at one time or another because that's what we were used to, so it was "normal". More and more people are refusing to reenact the trauma they've experienced early in life. This is as it ought to be, obviously.

◆◆◆

Giants are just one piece of the puzzle in our search for truth—albeit a huge one. Without the acknowledgment of the simple fact of Giants, nothing else is going to make a shred of sense in the overall understanding of the universe—thereby rendering true knowledge on the part of people who don't pursue this question incomplete...

Shapes in the clouds exist solely off of the memory of what has been—of this, I am more and more convinced. It isn't your imagination or pareidolia—what you are seeing in a cloud was there and happened at some point in the past.

There is absolutely no reason why clouds would take the form of a face, for instance, unless at some point that face was really there sometime in the past (for however long a length of time for the image to be intact enough on the ethers to be revealed by the clouds).

> *We imprint the ethers by everything we do;* the more we do a particular thing *(and especially in the same place),* the more we imprint the template of reality in that pose or (dis)position.

So, as above, so below: Giants being bigger beings than us would entail them making a bigger (albeit more sparse) physical imprint with more than likely a deeper impact or impression compared to humans. If the measurement of time is relative to the size of one's physical being, then in the Giants' world, their last cataclysm happened just recently enough that bodies in the ice are still subject to decomposition. To us, it may have been thousands or hundreds of thousands—perhaps millions—of years ago, but those bodies are still there waiting for discovery, acknowledgement, admittance.

So, if the momentum of actions leave their mark "upon the ethers" then it stands to reason that, because of the wide sweeps made by huge beings, their movements could appear in the very atmosphere that just happens to have clouds. These clouds reveal the momentum of Giants' action in highly charged states; they are a memory of the past in the atmosphere.

A linear, concrete example of all this could be, and this happens quite a bit in the photos I see on Google Earth: In the ocean or otherwise large bodies of water, many times schools of fish will be photographed outlining the carcasses of Giants beneath. They tend to hover, when undisturbed by man's presence in the ocean, in and around the skeletons and petrified remains of Giants—I've seen too many photos to not see this as occurring this way. And, in so doing, the fish at times, are the only things that make the Giants stand out as Giants at all.

In places imbued with strong emotions and trauma, we have observed those energies to manifest in the form of ghosts, apparitions, phantoms, or spirits. I liken the Giants, spirits, or ghosts to be like the elementals: nature spirits. Some of the giants were so humongous, they would easily cover an entire region of the map where they died.

Let's say the ghosts of Giants haunted the area that they died in; the haunting would be more dispersed and perhaps indirect, not concentrated with very pointed things happening within a confined area. Plus, all who died either on that Giant in the same cataclysm or anytime thereafter add to the memory and the activity swirl (like a carbon footprint) of a place. As this goes on, how much energy is accumulated that gives off a particular signature of vibration according to the kinds of activities that took place in that space?

The Earth is a graveyard: plain and simple. The Earth is built out of Giants of all sizes: Titans, nephilim, angels, watchers, devils, demons, jinn, religious warriors, archons and so on. Of course, the Earth is partially composed of deceased humans of all sizes, too.

The size of the first wave of Giants known as the Titans were of such immense proportions that they literally could not be seen by beings who were the same size we are now—that's a big "if" beings our size existed here and then...

Then, there is the revelation that our dimension (3D) appears to have been manifested or "unscrolled" merely to imprison demons? But this is hardly a new idea.

Imagine—if you will—the planet Herself as a Living Entity (which She is, of course). All planetary and star systems are living entities with a few exceptions, like the Moon or Nibiru. Just as there are robots or "non-player characters" (NPCs) in the human world as well as the principle of 'as above, so below,' in all systems larger and smaller the manifestations of consciousness are very similar across systems .

And, by the way, this also is not news; the Earth a Living Being—this is what every baby knows!

And, this planetary system, this Living Being Earth, that bears children—how big do you think her offspring would be? Even if this planet is as small as they claim it is, Her children would be too big for us to see as Living Beings who are mobile. But, these beings have existed in legend and myths no doubt sprung from seeds of truth that—if even just five percent of Giant stories were true—we'd still have Giants staring back at us from the camera lens of the satellites for Google Earth.

Going back to the idea of 3D being fashioned to imprison demons—it does make a lot of sense.
Much of the time life just doesn't feel good: death, disease, madness, obsession, pain, loss, suffering, grief, addiction, mental illness and physical disability seem to be part and parcel of life; we have only to look forward to the entropy at which it is inclined as the pinnacle

crowning achievement for the culmination of physical lifetimes in a body that cannot transmute us.

So, then it goes back to the truth that we are not our bodies and Western thinking does not acknowledge this simple fact. We have never been our bodies—*because if we were only that we would not have the cognition or the will that stems from having consciousness and a wherewithal.* We would not dream at night if we were only our bodies; consciousness outside of this awareness of the soul and spirit would not exist.

Now, maybe—just maybe—we really could be just dreaming robots with a preprogrammed descent into flesh and a mapped toggle switch: yes/no, multiple choice "fill in the scantron, please," auto-pilot life with an "illusion of (having numerous) choices." And maybe to some degree that last part is true but it does not matter.

We can only live one life at a time—which is not to say we don't live many lives simultaneously because (through this experience of sentience itself) it's clear to me that:

> ***I go where my conscious awareness goes. And, attention makes things real.***

Our internal world is just as real as the external world. Our inner space is hardly acknowledged though just as important as the outside world—if not more so.

◆◆◆

While I do believe the Giants were real and lived many, many times for longer periods throughout history and prehistory than we have any real clue about, I think it may be difficult to prove "scientifically" since—for all intents and purposes—*all* of the dirt and rock of Earth was once part of a Giant: a flesh and blood being at one time or another. I simply cannot stress this enough.

What I'm about to reveal to you, and which will give you ways to arrive at similar—if not the same—conclusions yourself, will certainly elicit a strong opposition from others. These conclusions are human interpretations of what the observing camera eye of Google Earth is taking a picture of...

What I find astounding, like I said before, is, if it were not for all the stories, folklore, myths, scripture and sacred texts talking about Giants, I might not have believed any of what I'm seeing on the program! But, being as how some of what I'm seeing on Google Earth is lining up with ancient texts, it's difficult to dismiss this as anything but revelation.

To go along with what I'm seeing, texts such as the following are difficult to ignore:

According to Gábor Kósa (2018),

> The watchers are not angelic figures, since they are none other than the demons captured in the first major battle between the two realms prior to the establishment

of the universe; and the creation of the cosmos was, among other elements, necessary to establish a suitable prison for the demonic forces who were not killed during this first battle. Those who were killed also played an important role: they became construction bricks in this huge endeavor, especially in the formation of the firmaments and the earths....Thus, the defeated demons had a double function in the construction of the cosmos: if dead, they were used to form the universe; if alive, they were imprisoned in the buildings partly built from their fellows. The cosmos itself had a double function: it served as a gigantic prison to hold the captured demons, and, at the same time, it served as a colossal hospital to heal the wounded, i.e. mixed, light particles. These two simultaneous purposes are explicitly mentioned together in the Coptic and Chinese sources. (p. 149)

Giants are everywhere—all over the planet—and they can easily be recognized as such. In fact, many of the tiny islands in the middle of nowhere in every large body of water in the world have visible evidence of Giants and, in certain places, indicates usually either a massive world-wide cataclysm like meteors or a great global battle taking place.

Figure 6. (Google, 2011, February 24) Many Giants died with their mouths opened wide as if they were in mid-scream.

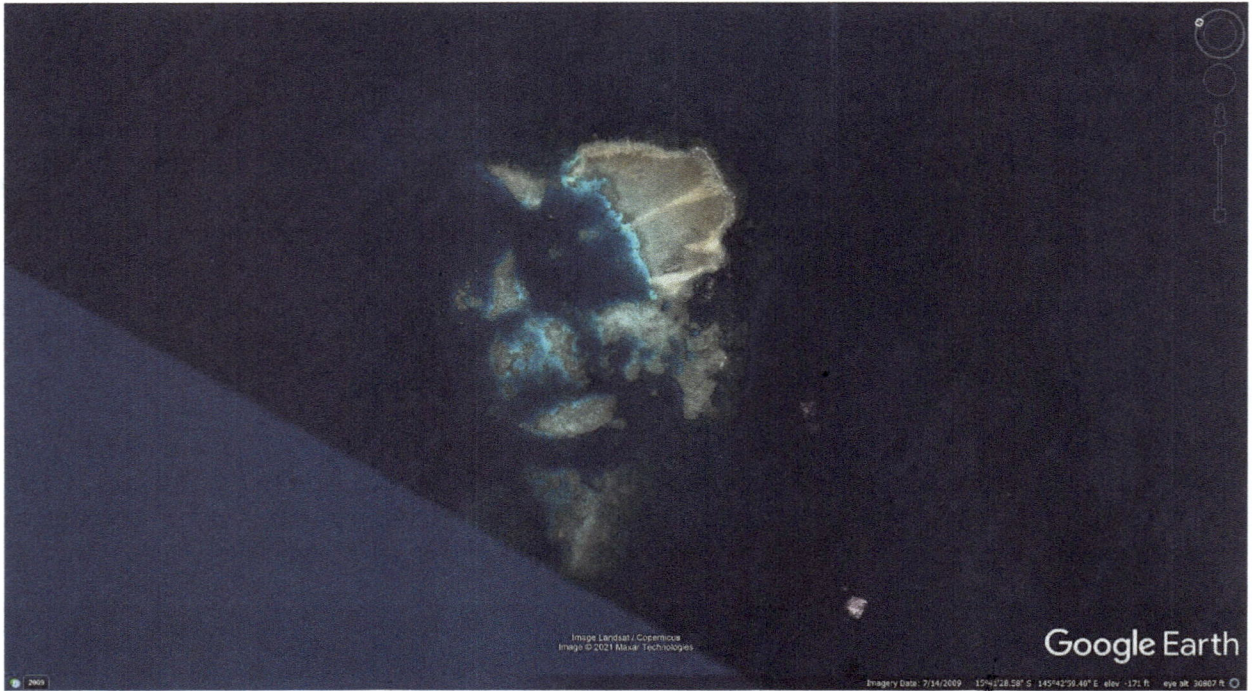

Figure 7. (Google, 2009, July 14) At times, evidence of Giants is just too obvious.

Figure 8 (2009, February 3). You can easily see the face(or half of it) of this giant on the top of Heard Island.

Figure 9. (Google, 2007, March 30). Not only a Giant above sea level, but a bigger Giant's face in the water

Figure 10. (Google, 2013, December 27). See the row of teeth?

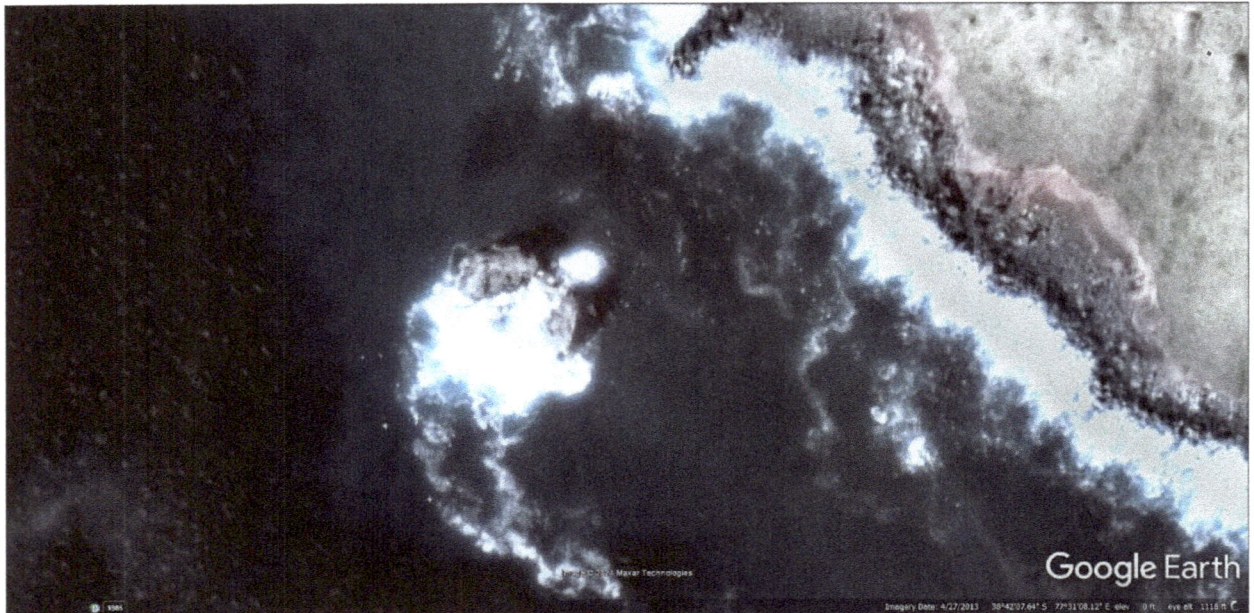

Figure 11. (Google, 2013, April 23) Mouth is gaping wide open. You can even see the legs underwater!

Figure 12. (Google, 2016, March 1) From one of the most isolated islands on Earth. The Giant's face extended out much more than readily appears. Or, it is two heads.

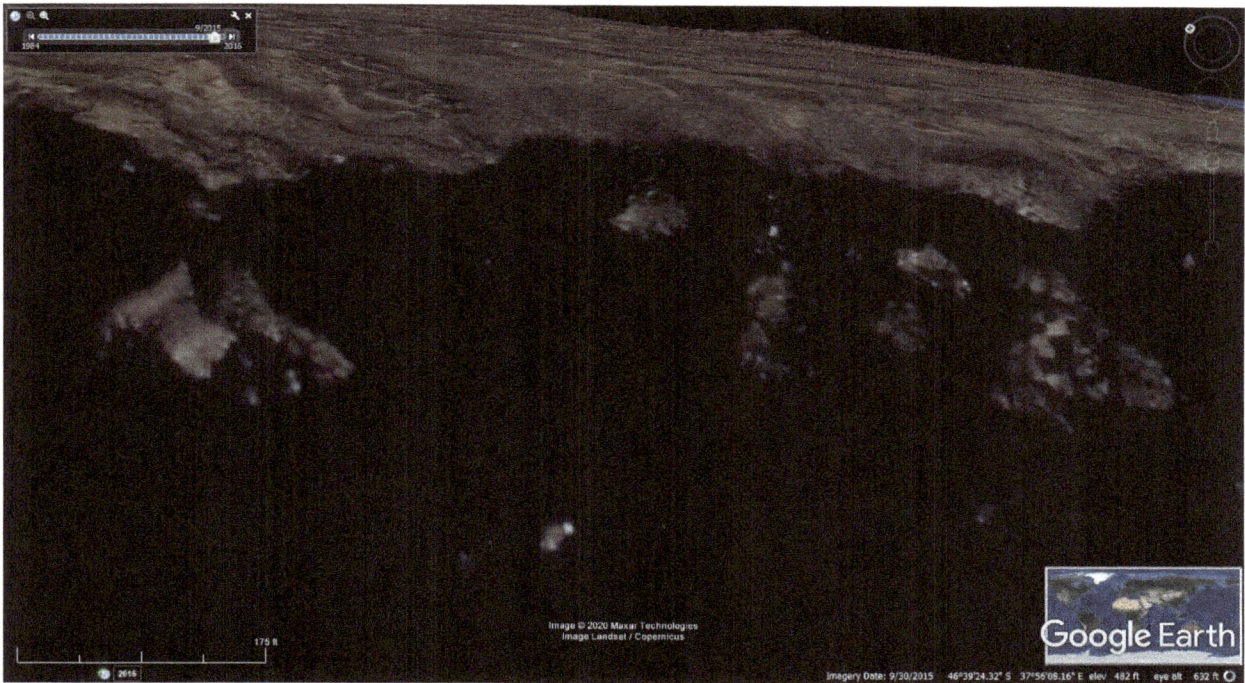

Figure 13. (Google, 2015, September 30) Faces at a cliff on a remote island.

Figure 14. (Google, 2005, December 9) Look closely at the water above the island, the island flows out of the Giant's mouth. Or, it looks like the lower jaw broke loose at some point to float to the top. Turns out, many islands formed in a similar fashion.

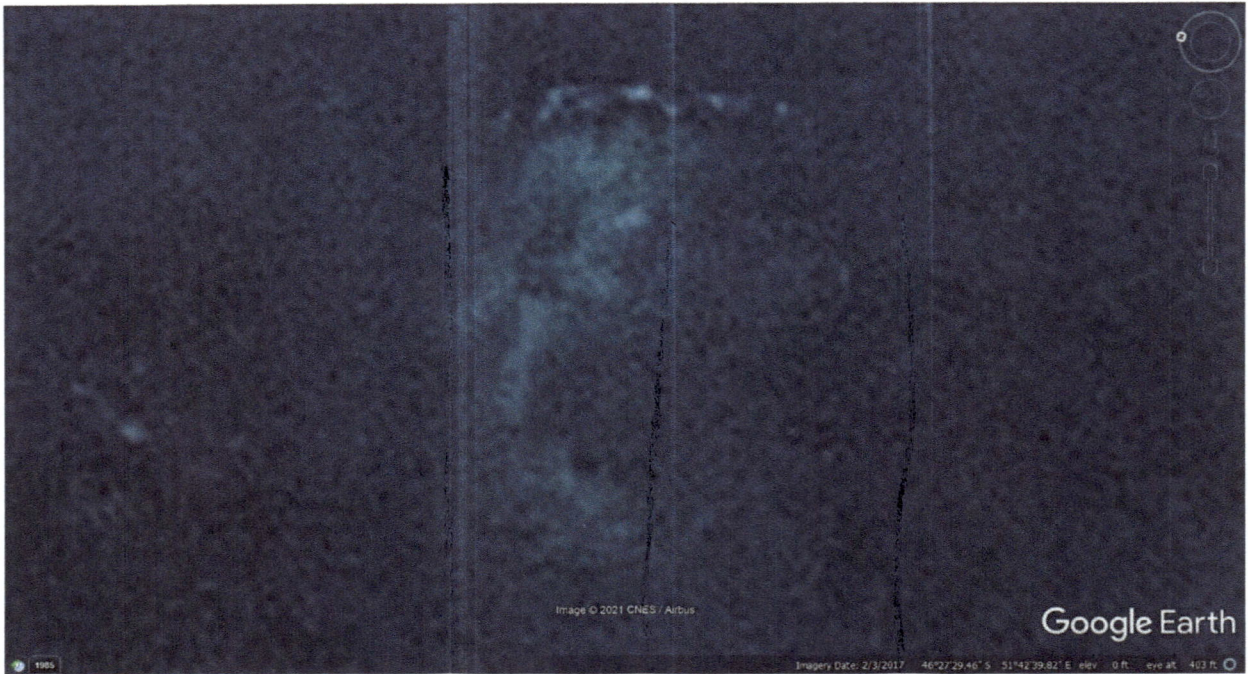

Figure 15. (Google, 2017, February 3) Head under the water.

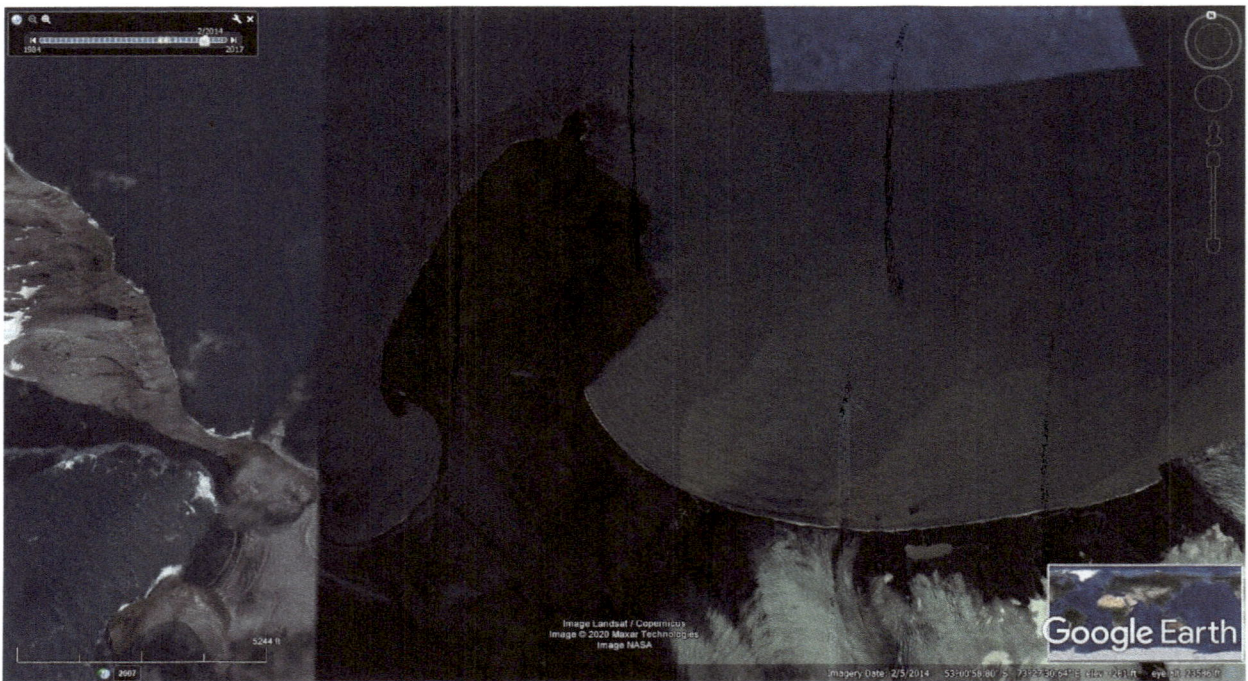

Figure 16. (Google, 2014, February 5) On Heard and McDonald Islands.

Figure 17. (Google, n.d.) Some of the best visual evidence of fingers.

Figure 18. (Google, 2006, February 14) Didn't I see a variation of this in a *Life Magazine* from last century?

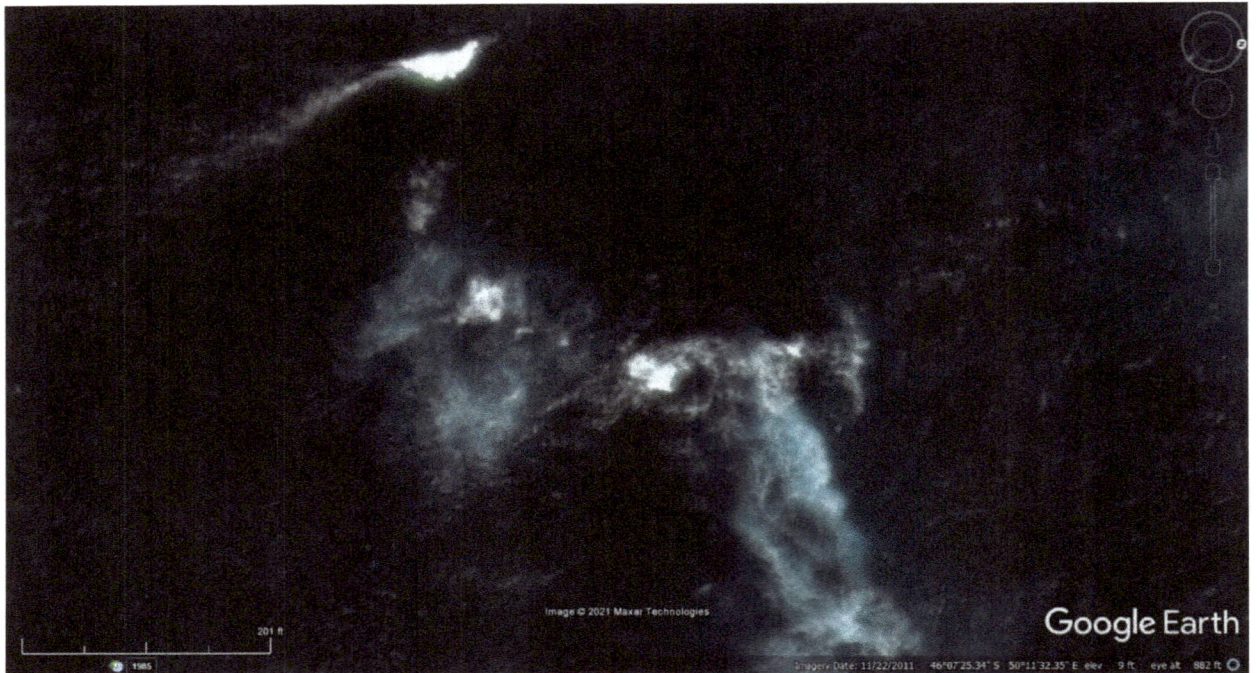

Figure 19. (Google, 2011, November 22) Two or three Giants: one is headless but appears to hold a head in his hand.

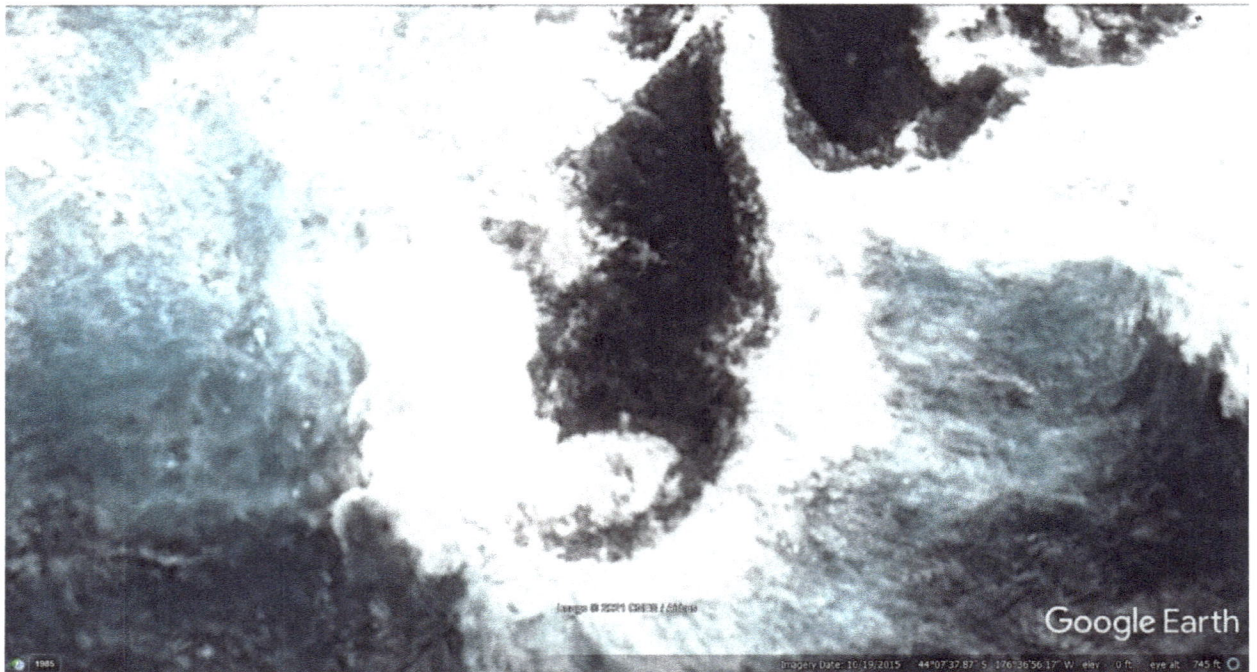

Figure 20. (Google, 2015, October 19) Petrified skull.

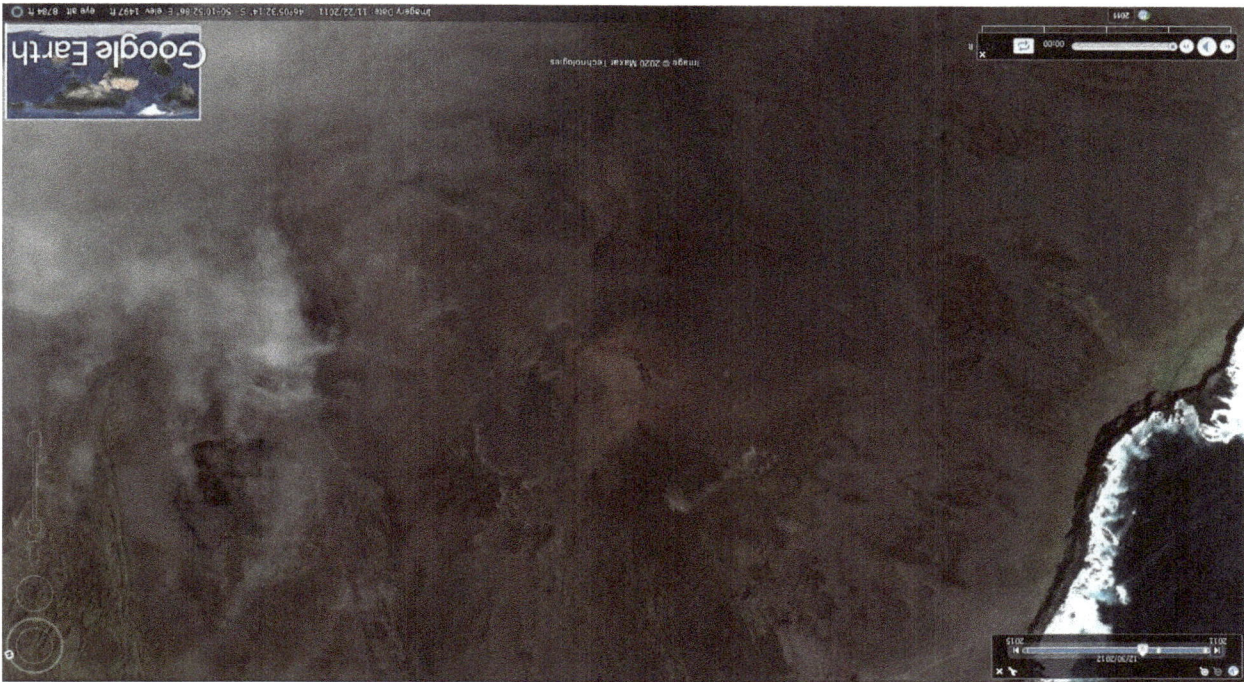

Figure 21. (Google, 2011, November 22) Head of Giant, teeth and eyes seen.

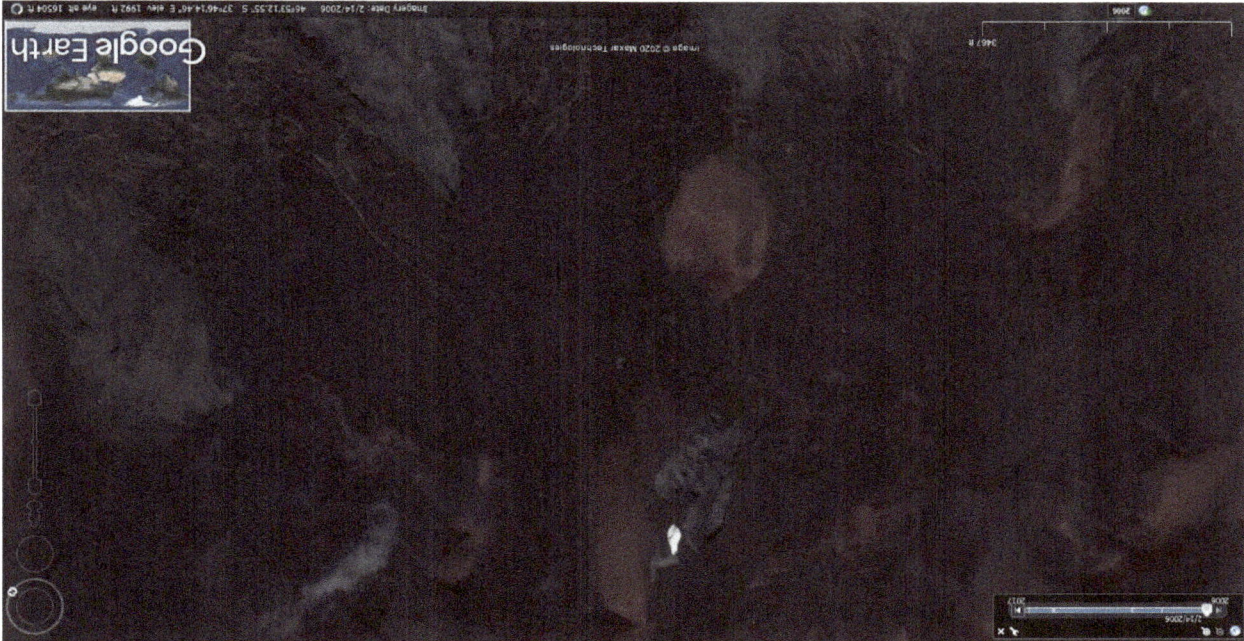

Figure 22. (Google, 2006, February 14) Appears like a head and two Giants holding each other.

Figure 23. (Zoom Earth, n.d.) Giant in ice or clouds on Zoom Earth.

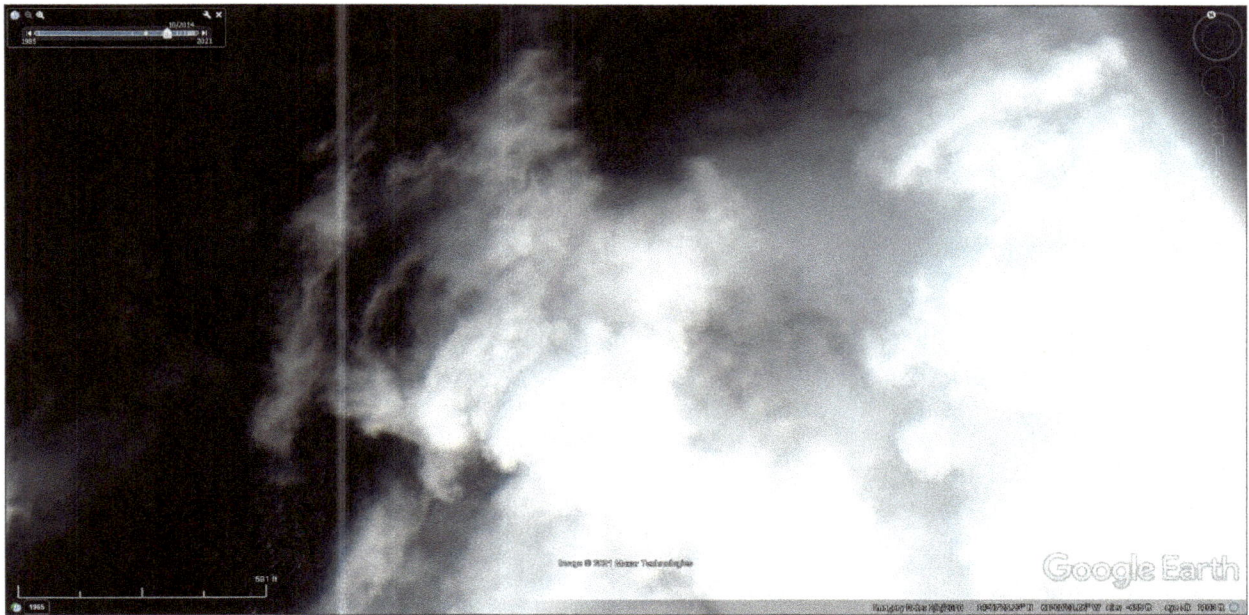

Figure 24. (Google, 2010) Several figures in these clouds.

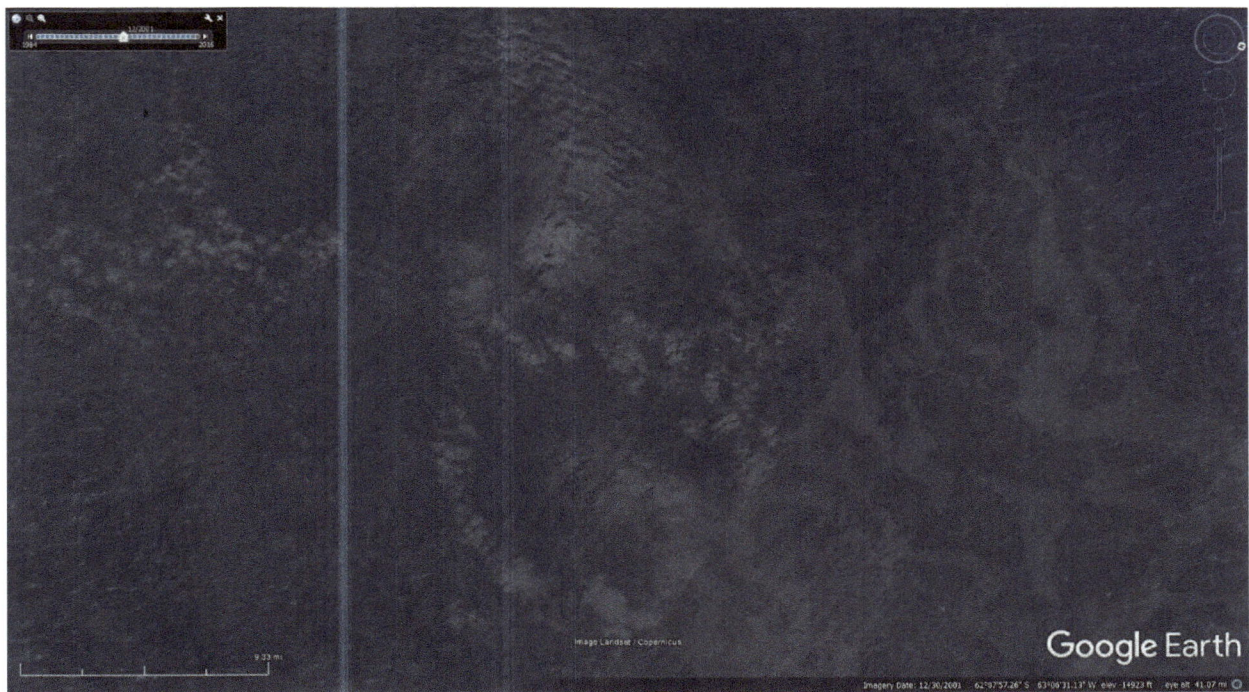

Figure 25. (Google, 2001, December 30) Even the ice preserves memories of what happened in the water.

Figure 26. (Google, 2005, December 11) Looks like a Giant reaching his hand up.

Figure 27. (Google, 2007, March 30) Clearly, these are the fingers of a Giant.

These phenomena couldn't have been caused by volcanoes—not yet. Not until after the Titans perished did the Earth utilize physical matter from their physical bodies—not until then were there volcanoes.

I realize that I am making fantastical claims with no scientific "proof"; however, nothing could have prepared me for what I was to find all over Google Earth.

And, let's face it: science easily has the capacity to be just as whack as woo but in the opposite direction. Science is just as closed, limited, and rigid as woo is too open: all inclusive and too loose. The need for science to rely solely on the five senses and to qualify their lab results as the Truth of Gospel is just as pathological as woo is for being nebulous, intuitively ascertained, and lacking cohesion or coherence.

I want to be as clear as possible when I say that Giants are any place you look, any mountain you see, any field, any pasture, any valley—anywhere. The entire landscape is composed of giants. In fact:

All Matter in 3D is derived from Flesh.

This is why the Word is so intertwined with Flesh—there's a mystery to be solved here because things do not add up as they are! Not that I can prove it, no, but the evidence is right there.

And with all that science concludes to be true, limits more of our understanding of everything than what we actually do know for sure about anything.

I am not trying to qualify the following as proof—absorb this book objectively and draw your own conclusions.

I feel this knowledge in my bones and I know it to be the Truth. After having the revelation of this, it's the only thing that makes sense as to how this 3D world came to be—how matter is formed at all.

One is born with a body only. How does anything else get here in this dimension?

Why do you think they say space smells like steak? Astronauts also report that space smells like "gunpowder, seared steak, raspberries and rum," as well as "ozone, hot metal and fried steak" and "pleasant sweet smelling welding fumes" (Ritschel, 2020).

We get to experience the impermanence of entropy every time we come and go into and out of this dimension and we are reborn into a new incarnation. The entire process feels forced and fated in a way that mimics a lack of control over the lucid dream.

Are we not told, over and over, that we are the ones who can create our reality and live a better dream—if we so choose? So why is it that we cannot complete the process by actually evolving? In a natural way.

◆◆◆

All one has to do is read an ancient text like *the Enuma Elish*: the story of Marduk and his battle with Tiamat.

The takeaway from that story is that Marduk is the hero—he was triumphant in his quest to control Tiamat.

I don't understand why Marduk's actions are so elevated by himself and his followers when it's clear to me that, in the message, is an undercurrent of trans-humanistic and technological mastery over Nature.

Marduk reigning over Tiamat is something that I can't understand from a perspective that's anything but linear and limited to 3D existence—it only makes sense if one were to negatively impact this dimension enough for it to maintain as 3D as what Marduk has apparently done. If the balance shifts towards the good, however, perhaps it will no longer be 3D.

Does it make sense to have something operate independently outside of itself? No, the mechanics of a thing—the workings—are on the inside.

Life, itself, operates from the emanations of the ghost in the machine—not by proxy and not remotely.

At the rate they are hollowing the planet out, Earth will only be fit to be "driven" by a stronger force quite like the Moon and Nibiru—dead celestial bodies, transitioned from being a Living Organism in the Macros. All the Living Planets are Giants as well; that is until someone decides to conquer, reign, and rule all that is under his feet: leech the land and its water and poison the air and bury toxic waste in the ground.

We've done this all before. And the outcome now is no different. All we need to do is remember, acknowledge, and not be in denial of the destruction of the Earth and its people: how it has all ended for us before, in mass trauma unfolding well beyond our control.

If not by the planet Herself or the movements of the stars (which both seem by way of providence), then it is by the plots and plans of man to erase "the enemy," who is anyone who has numbers on their side—saved not merely for political foes or those in squabbles for land at face value.

Because the fight for territory has never been about housing the people. Besides military strategy, it has always been about what natural resources are beneath the land—be it water, gems, minerals or—as pivotal to this particular epoch—fossil fuels.

So, Earth has—in the past—been pelted with comets, asteroids, meteors causing catastrophic loss of life; this caused massive tsunamis and shifted the poles, which threw the planet off its axis. That, in turn, started the seasons. Before this time, the Earth was oriented towards what was then the Black Sun, Saturn, which at the time was Earth's Sun and source of life.

Oh, and I don't apologize for feeling suspicious about much of what is handed to us as part of our heritage as sentient beings on the planet—or, as in this case, well before.

Don't you think that we've been under unlawful reign and, as individuals and, especially, as a group, we've been geared towards some of the wrong things: like the pursuit the money, which, in turn, produces billionaires who are currently buying up huge parcels of land because someone wants to ride this planet after they hollow Her out to provide their fuel to then take them to space so they can land on other planets and take those over of their resources, too?

Don't you folks get it? You are their fuel, also.

As long as these billionaires, for example, can get away with not paying income tax or having their way paid to space via public funding it's just going to get worse. Less and less funding for social programs, school programs—it's all going away toward a dim transhumanist future: one that they are happy to let you work your ass off for so they can grab your social security benefits, too; go ahead and die when you are no longer making money for them. And you never even get to find out what you were born to do.

We are swayed and dissuaded from our purpose. Freedom is only for those that can afford to buy it; there is absolutely no other way to attain it unless you live in the bush and are completely or almost completely self-sufficient—even then you didn't start from nothing; if you did then you were raised in the bush and all this information is redundant.

Madmen are setting about and are controlling every aspect of your lives. Is that what you want? Every waking and sleeping moment is monitored, cataloged, and stored for use later at a convenient time.

The bottom line is: whether or not Giants were real, the Google Earth images indeed merit investigation. If these are not Giants, then there are definite artifacts out there that are waiting to be discovered. But, with all the imagery taken over the past half century from satellites, it's unlikely that the elite don't already know these things exist—no matter what these things are.

Chapter 1: *The Ninth Circle: The Observer of Objective Reality

Etheric Impressions of What 'Is'

Throughout the spatially lengthened and heightened measure of All Places—in the depth and from the breadth of immeasurable means, in gossamer and finer fractal fields—open ended revolutions spin. Such that they might multiply in omnidimensional quantum unfoldment and entanglement—and stretch in magnitude, velocity and distance.

The stretched expansion of the lung's inhalation moves along the meridian lines of fire until the synapses in tandem produce a current up the chain which goes lighting up the way through your neural pathways.

You've watched this in the way of stacked-up fractals: the exact workings in order-linearly. It isn't like when Creation speaks Life, when flames that leap and dance interact extralinearly—that's what an agreement or recognition is. That is a harmonious chiming of two or more, from any monad(s) in that realm.

One would have to catch up to the memories of past events to experience the manifest thought. But, it can only be experienced by proxy. Anytime that you must re-member—rather than experience the experience—it tells of a different sort of copyright! This leads to automatons, clones, drones, and bots. "Clone rights" wars, indeed! (It's alright, that was meant to be absurd.)

So, consciousness begins on the subatomic level with gluons and quarks and etheric dark matter—Her pregnancy, of many forms, had taken to the incarnate and in them, not so sentient Spirits. And no Soul—no memory or experience. Keep in mind that in this description of the creation of life and consciousness, which is well beyond antiquity, All is new that Forms from the matter left by explosions between shining stars. Consciousness exists before anything or anyone could bear witness to it. That is, pay attention to the matter. How could anyone or anything exist before matter ever formed to watch it happen? This could well be a logical fallacy.

Whatever is the matter that formed itself? Why, the stuff of Stars! Photons, atoms, ions, the space between (seemingly empty to) your eyes' spectrum of sight, and so on. Hearing the lights and seeing the sounds is something you are predisposed to do—something that was a natural function at one time—but black magicians (scientists) have flipped switches in the genome of the latest few humanoid-version prototypes; they mostly turned off switches that would link you to multidimensional fields in your conscious, active state.

Ghosts in the machine, to be sure—output is naturally high and the channels are few, such new spirits without memory or experience of anything; it's like a shot in the dark, needle in a haystack such that not even one monkey "gets it."

And, being the social animals that we are, our need for acceptance within our tribe is pivotal to the point of sacrificing our base judgment: just to be counted. Your Creator is not necessarily your Benefactor, nor has He Created since the First, a Beneficent Presence.

Free Will is a coveted yet dubious thing. We are only allowed it insofar as the switches that are turned on—if we had full capability, at full capacity, it is doubtful we would have received "free will"; the term is a misnomer, anyhow. At the level of this dimensionality (3D), there is nothing free nor of endless potentiality about it. It still operates as a closed Logos, in its figure-eight configuration.

And, given that we would exercise our Free Will in order to give allegiance to governmental closed systems of eventual totalitarian agencies, shows a lack of judgment far beyond any justification for "ignorance."

What is simple is still uncomplicated but agreeing for the sake of agreement is convoluted—it causes us great cognitive dissonance and trauma as a species.

The trauma and pain of war and cataclysm reverberates to this very day—it shows in how we treat one another with intolerance, judgment, and callousness. We will squabble over our skin colors and racial differences while forgetting the fact that to begin with, we are all part of the same human race.

For complacency, you have traded your freedoms and want to breach the barrier of space because you think you can control what's beyond it.

But what mankind fails to realize or care about, is that attempting to break through the glass ceiling will prove futile in our efforts to gain access to and build a stronghold on some extraterrestrial real estate:

We cannot leave. Not in this form, not in this dimension.

My! Don't we look foolish to the eyes that peer upon you every day from a lofty space out in the cosmos! Laugh with a mighty guffaw!—you may get the sense that you're imprisoned here on the planet; yes, this is true. Or worse yet, think that you are somehow protected by being here under a dome. But you really can't expect that it's to "keep the crazies *out*"!

What this solar system—nay the Universe—*doesn't* need is for its genetically modified cells spreading to other parts of the body of the Universe, infecting(terraforming) everything it contacts. It is as simple as that!—seeing as Earth not long ago was a veritable graveyard. Even Mars didn't see such decomposition, what with Mars' atmosphere being stripped from it. And Venus—there is still decomposition happening there, now.

Venus' flash was not so extreme—only enough to make Venus release her water from within herself (the planet was almost blanched but dryly—flash-steamed if you will) and then the displaced water as cloud cover acts as constant condensation/precipitation (greenhouse effect).

◆◆◆

Why would an established entity such as the Smithsonian Institute go to lengths to destroy physical artifacts like skeletons of Giants if Giants weren't real?

Because an acknowledgement of their skeleton bones opens a can of worms that leads to another bigger can of worms that leads to yet another bigger can of worms and so on until the truth about the existence of Giants is readily recognized by average people merely observing the landscape on Google Earth and with a bigger piece of the truth people seriously begin questioning the bigger mysteries of human kind's very existence.

But, the main reason why the truth about Giants is covered up is control: control of government and church over the masses—plain and simple.

Can't have people believing in Giants because that would be one of the threads that would unravel the whole angular lattice-work structures of interwoven concocted, convoluted Evolution myths and Creation myths. Basically, it's a Luciferian agenda on the part of the powers that be.

After all, it *is* a Luciferian agenda that runs the establishment; this is not to say that everyone in the establishment is down with the sickness of this agenda. Most know nothing of the plans of their employers, military, or government. They are just unwitting obedient sheep—being led to believe they're doing what they are doing for good—but this is not the case. Because many of us want to do the right and good thing on a small scale in our everyday lives, we don't see the overall agenda that's part of a much bigger picture.

At the end of the day, the way everything is run maintains to keep the bloodline families in pocket, in power, in control, and indoctrinating through their academic institutions with their "truths," their histories rewritten at their whim. The Great Reset is part of this repetitious planned action—and the cycle repeats and repeats generation after generation.

Sure, there are seeds of truth to each belief system—but the knowledge that Giants roamed the Earth even once, at only twice our size contradicts just about every edict that these governing offices and belief systems depend on for the "legitimacy" of their narrative. Just wait until the truth about Giants' real size comes to full light and it blows peoples' belief systems to bits. Perhaps this revelation is meant to happen as in the aftermath of our existence we can now be healed and transformed by the truth about our history—about the Earth's herstory.

Truth will clear up the cognitive dissonance that we all suffer collectively from knowing there are things that are purposely withheld from us—likewise, truth will quell the feeling that we are being distracted from our purpose and being led to value some wrong things like the pursuit of money for instance, which has made many people rationalize just about any and every way of getting it.

You see: the reason why students are geared toward one pointed area in their field is not so they don't spread too thin—well yes that, too, but it's secondary to not giving anyone just the right amount of knowledge in many areas where a larger number of people will start putting things together and seeing the contradictions, the hypocrisy and the exclusivity and narrow mindedness that academia *can* condition people to have. Keep peoples' focus on this corner, right over here!—look close with laser-like tunnel-vision so that you don't catch the hink and jenk happening in your periphery.

This subtle form of control is done, also, to cut down the amount of people who are experts in more than one area—because that would definitely produce lots of people that know how to do lots of different things in order to, say, survive catastrophe, or come up with solid plans to overthrow an ever-encroaching dictatorship.

Or, even merely seeing how pigeon-holing oneself can be dangerously myopic giving one a shielded existence wherein the view of oneself becomes dysphoric and unrealistic: a caricature of itself (thus of oneself), rigidly adhering to "the way it's always been" or "the way it is"—and we get set in our own grooves and habits and quirks and they too become caricatures as extensions of our own selves.

If they can push people into one little tiny area of study, they'll be less capable with less knowledge to know what to do in a global crisis—like how to survive and live off the land. Their degrees in computational molecular biology or kernel code programming become useless!

Young people would benefit being taught how to live off the land—virtually no one is taught those things any more. And, it's all because it really does take a village to raise a child. But, the villages are now big, anonymous cities and the urban lifestyle is detrimental to every psyche in it—city life disrupts everything to one's dream cycles to there being too many strangers that no one knows and thus cannot readily or easily trust. Yes, it takes a village—not a metropolis.

I understand that I'm generalizing but what I'm trying to say is that not educating people in many areas of study breeds ignorance of what it means to really have to keep yourself alive in the world—the world in its natural state, anyway.

That's exactly why they are trying to do away with the world in its natural state; the powers that be are trying and vying even to control Nature itself. Genetically-modified organisms (GMOs) have threatened the entire food supply and farming grounds with roundup-ready faux seeds: punching holes in guts; shredding and fragmenting the body, mind and soul. It is not hard to see what is happening here! This is to get us slowly used to having fewer and fewer nutrients—this goes right along with a transhuman agenda. Replace the body parts with machinery little by little—metal and even plastic, circuit boards, nanobots.

The powers that be are trying to eradicate the animal part of ourselves; it cannot be done successfully without severe consequences—take out the animal in the human and you are left with a rag doll! The animal-in-human is wrapped up with the Soul and in turn, Memories.

It does not make sense to control Nature and to control the Human and seed genome—this sounds like a madman's attempt to control people, situations and outcomes. But I digress, Time will tell; there will be brave souls that will be able to scientifically prove the existence of Giants with DNA. If it's not already happening—it will happen soon.

What one ought to do with this information is study Google Earth yourself—while you still *can*. Each new version of Google Earth gets progressively harder to view interesting things and—most certainly—"questionable" things; a lot is now blurred or it's covered with endless filters and/or clouds. Don't study the browser version, study the downloadable version of Google Earth Pro.

Also, check out Zoom Earth! This is a browser application that shows strange-looking weather patterns of clouds which many times resemble humans (albeit fantastically larger than the current *homo sapiens* inhabiting the planet).

It is no secret that clouds and fog all roughly outline that which it covers. And, being that clouds and fog are made of water (and it's a well known fact that water holds memory), the idea that huge weather systems give telltale signs of past events is not so far-fetched. A good look at Zoom Earth will indicate that.

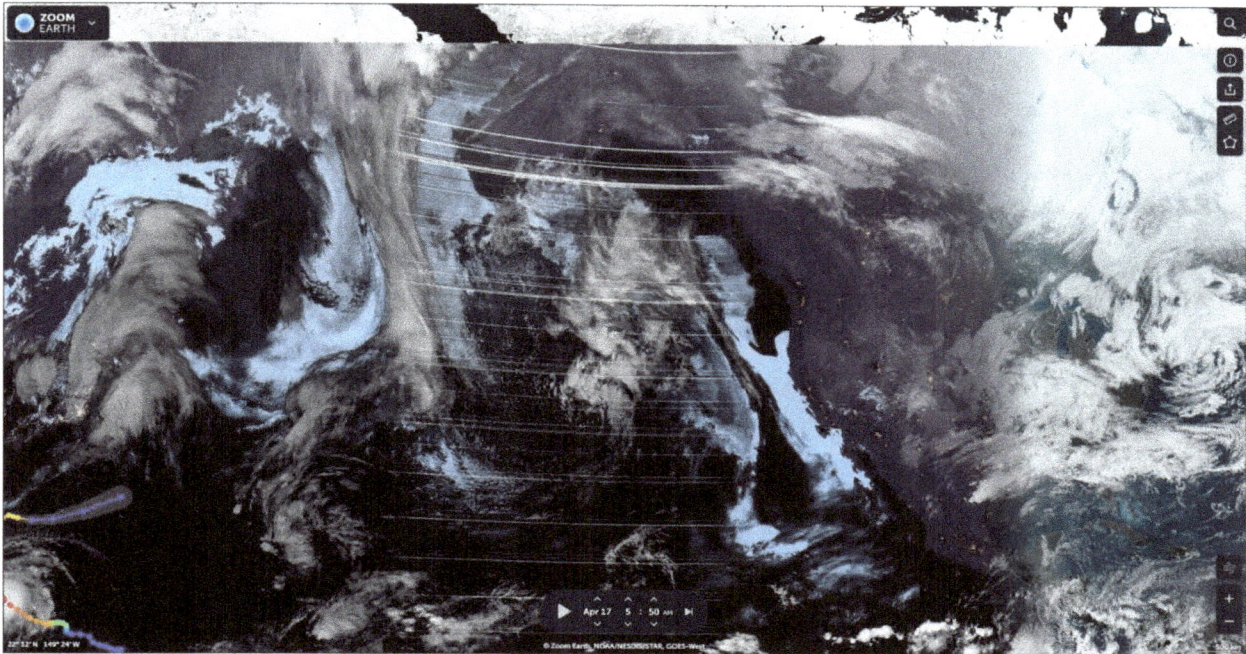

Figure 28. (Zoom, n.d.). Faces in the clouds.

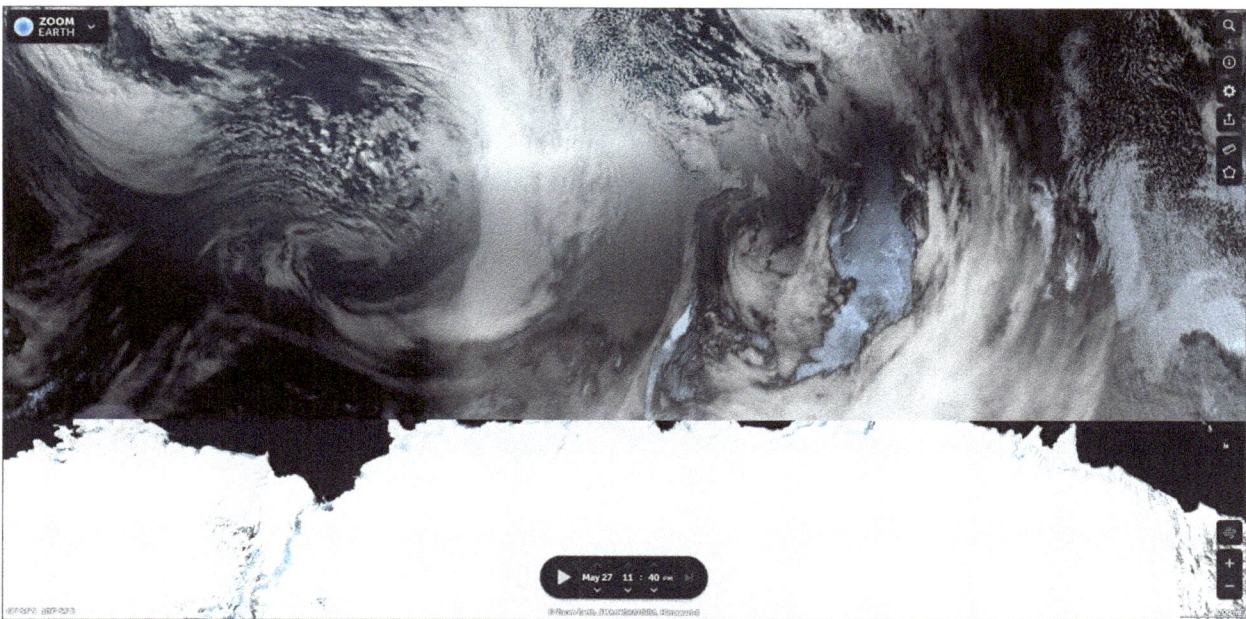

Figure 29. (Zoom, n.d.) Huge face with obvious eyes and teeth.

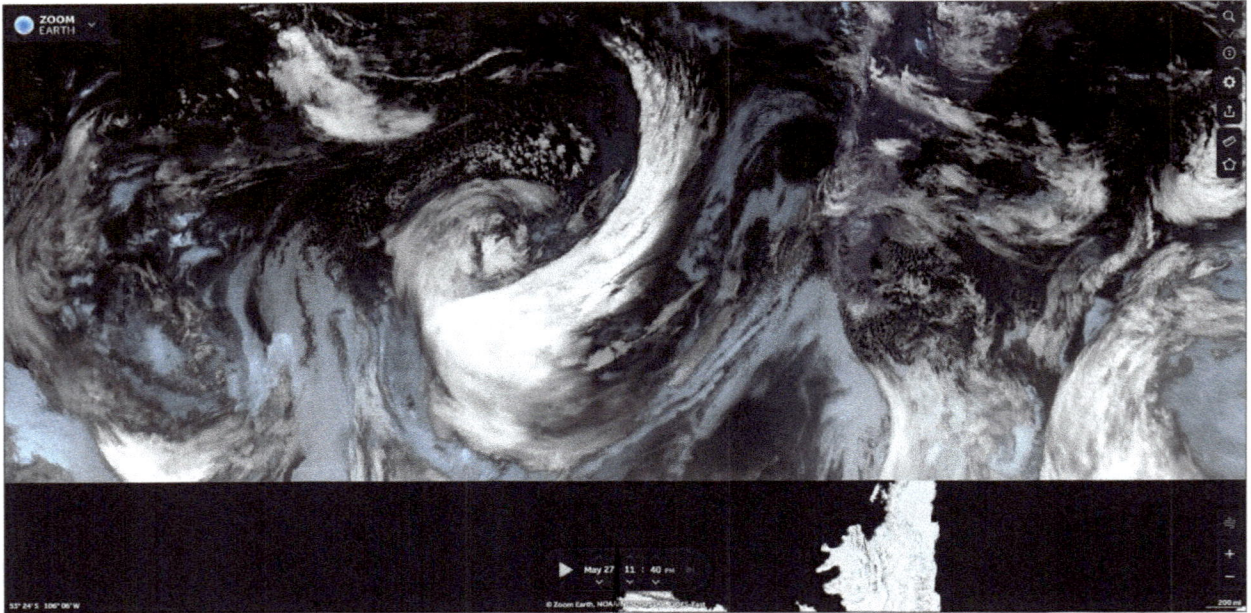

Figure 30. (Zoom, n.d.) More faces.

Figure 31. (Zoom, n.d.) Huge face with mouth open wide on right side.

Figure 32. (Zoom Earth, n.d.) Hands in the form of clouds reaching down to the ground in the center of the photo.

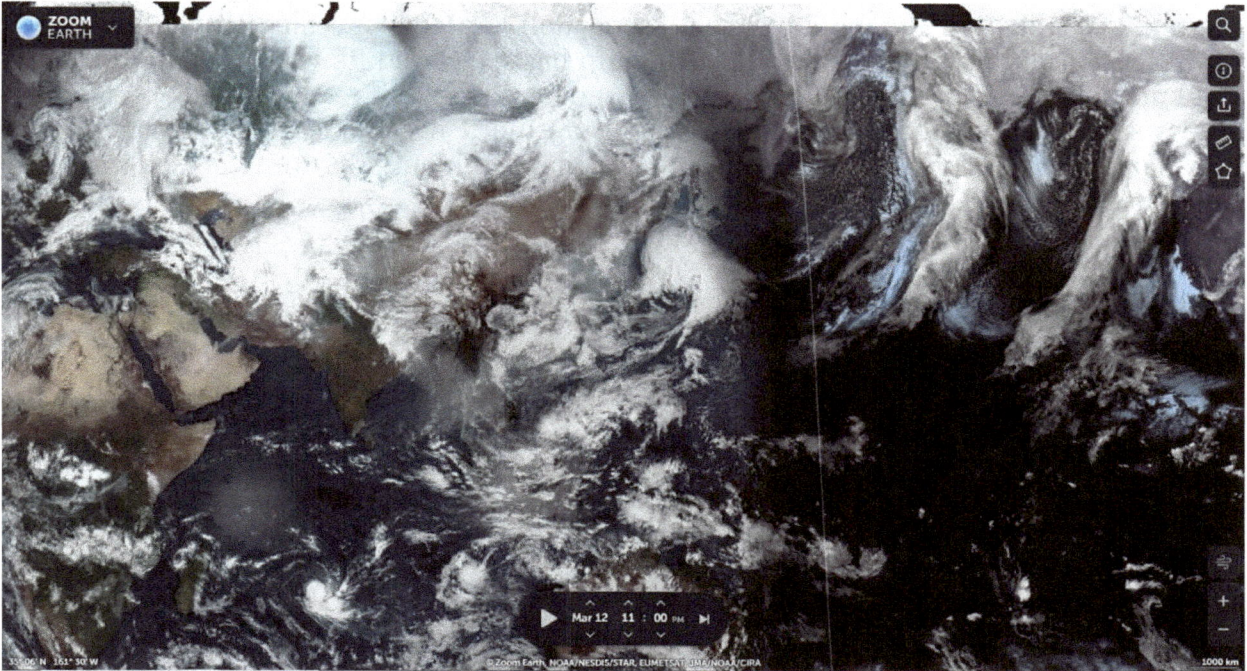

Figure 33. (Zoom, n.d.) Many faces of Giants.

Figure 34. (Zoom, n.d.) Giant on its side.

There is too much on Google Earth that seems deliberately concealed! If you have been paying attention over the years to how the app has narrowed its visual capabilities, you will know what I'm talking about. There is no good reason to have something blurred out unless something is being hidden! Most of the time if it's blurred (and not a military installation or similar) it is because it looks human—the only reason I can see for doing this is because it really *is* a human Giant.

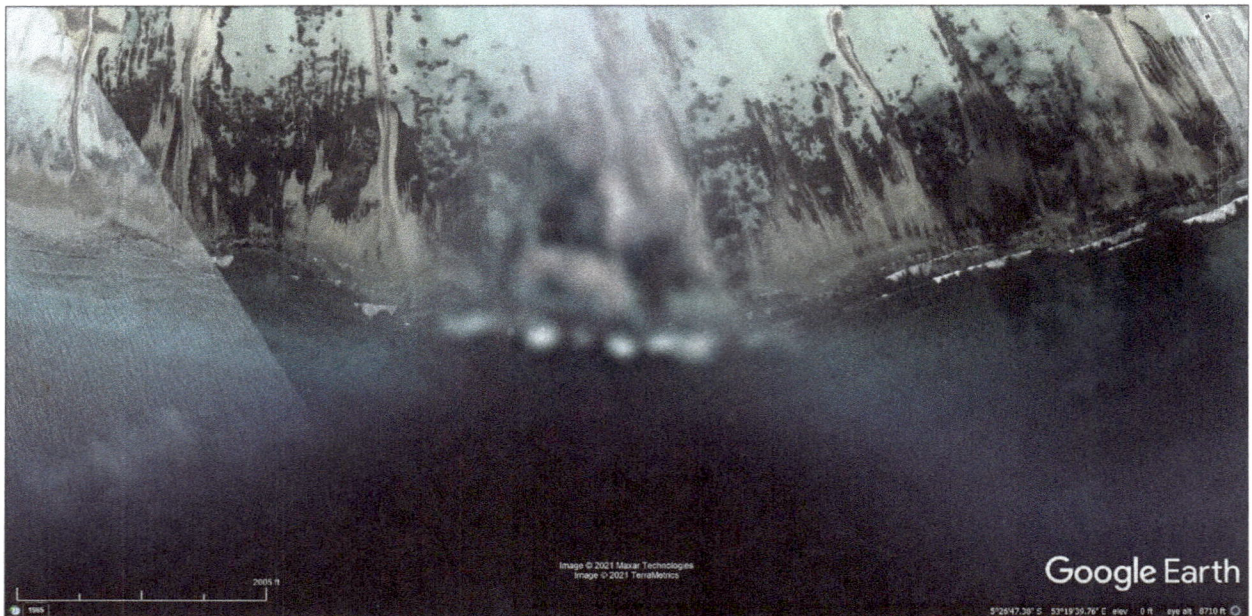

Figure 35. (Google, 2021) Things that are blurred out because they look human.

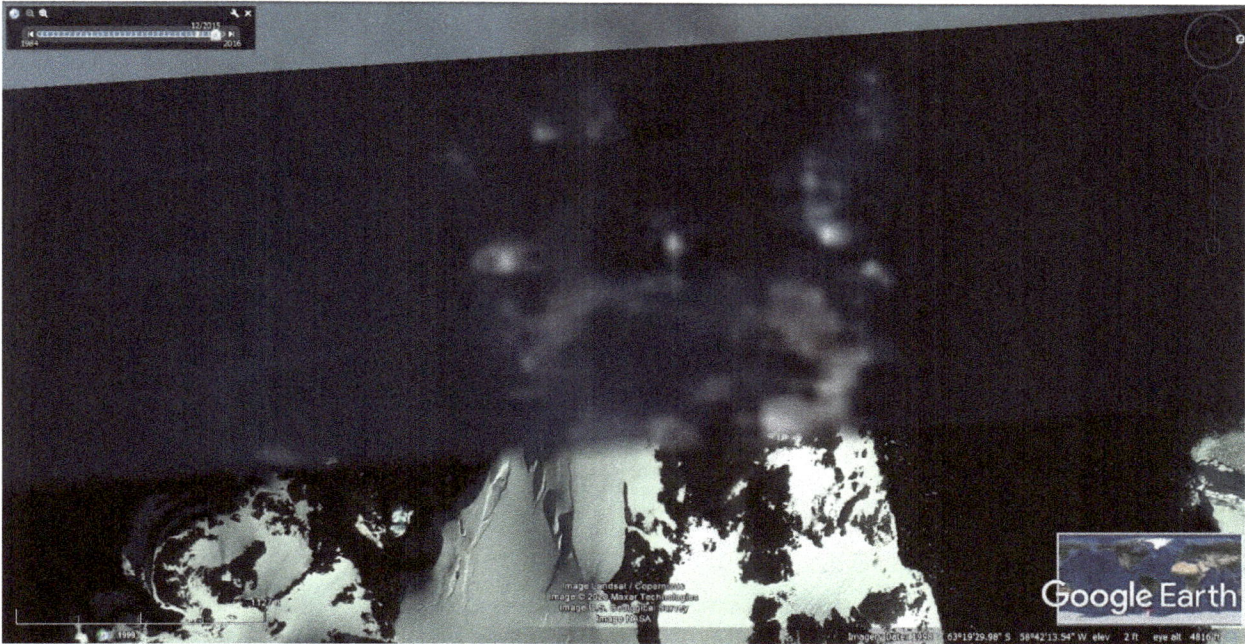

Figure 36. Google Earth (1998) Almost like 3D abstract art, stare long enough and the heads "pop out."

Figure 37. (Google Earth, 2015, December 13) Blurred face of Giant in the ocean.

Figure 38. (Google, 2012, January 13) Blurred Giant remains. See the legs towards the bottom of the photo.

No one can sensationalize the Truth because the Truth these days is sensational—counterintuitively—at least, from an experience where Truth is still a novel thing. In other words, Truth wouldn't be sensational if it was practiced as the norm!

Truth is only stranger than fiction when the audience is not used to truth being an automatic function of perception and response.

Here ya go!

Truth is only stranger than fiction when it's not practiced as the norm.

Our human arrogance will be our downfall every time! We are so self assured about the exact wrong things and faith wavers so greatly over things completely out of our ability or willingness to innerstand or overstand. We crystallize too soon—sealing in those old outdated beliefs we haven't updated since—say—high school or college that just do not apply anymore and have not been relevant since we formed the beliefs.

We stop creating new neural pathways in the brain by closing off our opinions, beliefs, and ways of doing things; we snap shut the ability to be open to new ideas—especially when it comes to taking advice from younger people.

Older people have a hard time heeding advice from *younger* people because older people think they've cornered the market on life experience—but, if that person's life experience is narrow, rigid, and with a minimal radius (that the young person may have already encompassed in life) then there will be no value or it will even serve as a warning to the younger person.

I know that, at some point years ago, I stopped looking to many older people for advice—knowing how biased their perception is because of a limited range of experience or they're fixed and rigid of thought. Many older people served more as a warning to me than not.

And, I'm positive that it's the same for a younger person looking at me saying to themselves "Yikes! What a warning! Don't wanna be like that!"

For a long time, I've viewed the younger and younger generations to be inherently more evolved and more intelligent than the previous generations—that's not the same as being more enlightened and advanced spiritually. However, many and more younger people are more advanced and enlightened on a spiritual level. Young people long before this point were already advanced beyond my generation before I even went to high school!

But, I come from a rigid and hard-headed generation.

This current Western civilization is so new but it is already so pronounced; one has to study the culture with all its pop culture and memes, advancements in technologies and sciences/business, all its art forms—everything about this culture for the past 100 years—*in utero*. That is probably why kids come out of the womb seemingly knowing how to do stuff mommy and daddy can't do—such as how to eventually come to coexist with technology. That and children—no doubt—have cellular memory of whence they came, probably as their great great grandparents on back who started this "industrial revolution" in the nineteenth century.

◆◆◆

The powers that be set up this rat race and you'll kill yourself for the convenience of being able to die early...hurry before the next guy does it!

We live our lives as if we were merely worker bees or ants—it's the flex on the part of the powers that be that was more or less coerced onto you, making you feel ashamedly responsible for something you have no part in until you conform because society dictates that you must have a list of things in order to be accepted.

The powers that be have systematically brought us down to the lowest common denominator as merely a possession for their use and misuse—if not *abuse*. Because when they are done using the best years of our lives, they discard us—the sooner the better because they will always tell certain folks to proliferate (such as the purpose of replenishing the military) so as to use up the next generation of fresh blood for their money generating wars of invasion and retrieval.

And, in doing this, we never get the chance to find out who we are ourselves and why we choose to incarnate on the Earth. People's purposes get run roughshod over by the time we can even form sentences. People are conditioned to be controlled and told what we "should" do.

◆ ◆ ◆

You will come to realize that the apparent overlapping of archetypes (such as of ancient mythologies) and of the signs of the stars (such as the Zodiac) is meant to show how everything in the universe is in motion and a fixed star is hardly bound in place.

Everything on this continuum is in a forward thrust—as much as "they, them, those"; the powers that be are trying to suspend this grand anime.

As far as Google Earth is concerned, you have to study it closely for Giants but sometimes they jump right out at you! There is evidence of missile fire as plainly seen as strange lines that crisscross the bottom of the oceans from Google Earth.

The cataclysm and warfare that has transpired on this planet has been extensive and it is really quite obvious to see if one looks at the planet looking straight down on the map of Google Earth: there are heads and hands...there are headless bodies by the hundreds of thousands—if not millions—of Giants throughout the Earth in all Her firmaments.

The most obvious place to see what remains to this day of the most intact of Giants' bodies is under the ice at the North and South poles. As well as the poles, most coastlines upon inspection will reveal Giants just off the shorelines, in the water.

You will need to play with the Timeline feature (clock icon showing "historical imagery") on Google Earth. I am without a doubt that this will prove to be quite revealing to those with open, yet discerning, eyes.

Chapter 2: *In the Pit: Starry Arms of Albion

The Black Sun was tinted with ultraviolet light and purple skies which showed Him in His sways as the Ancient of Days. The planets were conceived in Orion near the constellation Gemini, forged in the fire of the galactic center in the constellation Sagittarius, long having started their magnetic dance around the Black Sun, and it, around the galactic sun.

'Dreams are what we make them / And time does not abate them / Smile upon Creation / From every station'

Has this happened already? Or, is it a future memory—a panacea for my dreams as I sleep—these fleeting fully conscious thoughts just inside my head? Are they just inside my head or do my legs take me down that road I've walked for many miles into the seamless vanishing point of night? I feel my feet in my shoes but am I walking upon the air?

As I wondered this, I immediately began hovering and then going higher until I was looking down over the tops of trees. The plains stretched out before me and I was transported/teleported to where?

I was already there! A place I don't recognize—but I felt like I've been there before. Over the purple hills, over empty village squares, over the vast empty caves where the healing class used to synthesize stones and plants and sea life to create their alchemy in potions, tinctures, tonics, and balms.

The air is cool in the lowest of the atmospheres and the lightning all around illuminates the skies in one steady streaming light—so much lightning. The night sky is as bright as daylight. So much electricity and ozone.

We were—that is, our group was—to anchor a stone in Her stern: a Lightning Stone of Living Liquid Light. Ah, the Spinal Fluid of Stars, the Giants! Birthed in Living Waters of the Milky Way.

And, as sure as the Eye of Eta Carina stares at this scene which we have made our Home— albeit a temporary one—the sand finally stopped smearing the landscape, drifting into lower spaces and settling in vast sea beds.

For our ancient eyes, there was no discernible daylight from the night light seen because, in those times, our optical vision wasn't well defined. We could see blurry outlines of forms and colors as they blend into one another. But no faces, as we still had little wherewithal in conscious awareness.

And this was all before we could see well enough to assume light itself be associated with "good" and thus darkness associated with "evil"—just because you can see in light!

But, the light is actually to hide in. And, here's why: the light gives a thing being illuminated the very form in which it is seen because the appearance of form in light changes with the observation of the viewer. Period.

A general evolutionary step was to recognize self before you could recognize another—the spirit and the soul—newly born and grown together, yoked.

When things perceived were truly simultaneous, the sight you had was like looking through binoculars but looking at everything close up, around the room in the immediate environment. There was a blurry general sense of things but no definition to form. The form and figures from the astral planes were largely visible to your black light eyesight.

And, that is what we have molded. This is our creation: the thought that manifests the Shape into Form. And, we leap like flames to lick the fire and hammer hot glass that the volcanoes smolder—brimless are Her fiery lips. We wait for the pang of birth and slow thickly red heat of magma's quiet envelope—cut right from the mold and melded together and held sinew and steam and intrigued us from a dream.

Far to follow the form-fitted letters branded upon the ethers in simple omnitones, languages of light manifested as flashes of fiery light—with clean fiery slices of air, did they wear. Each and every utterance and groan of Creation to its appropriated Form. No Sword for the Sacred, profane name; we would call for them just the same, as there was No One here to see it so—no witness to testify, no stranger passer-by. No secret falls from High.

Into the shapeless darkness did orbit a cosmonaut of distract—the beacon that beckons wild to the heartbeat of Creation's child. The vapor and the ember to catalyze life in this earthen pot, while the chaff and the dross is drawn off. Polymer of plastic and metal of cloth may disguise to hide what light will not abide.

Yet, to be lit up to see the shell first covering thee. Seeing as you were the Light under the bushel! You were made self-aware but fragile: open yet guarded—so trusting yet contrarily so suspicious. Yours' was sprung from the yoke of restraint. Much too thin of skin and highly vulnerable—impressionable but volatile—no rein on e-motions and feelings are ever wavering. Your mind goes wandering and then you get lost for a moment and three hours later, snapping to—falling prey to subjugation, you are a living duality. See?

For the human is a truly wild beast and yet his instincts may fail him for the unraveling and flitting of the mind—never resting but in fits and starts enjoys an assured and secure groove of a dim self-awareness.

What commotion did render the magnetosphere to bend the light into lines, squares, cubes and dots? Only at angles do angels arc cutting with fiery feet across the ground—in as soft a landing as they could drop into from the path of comets.

And the Earth shuddered. Yes, She, in the wake did then see the many that swept in once the Moon became Sin and the blood as in a centrifuge separated from the life-giving light. Like statically-charged dust particles to a newly rubbed balloon.

Blood of heavy iron magnetized to the ground scattered, splattered and wasted—now mixed with sand, sun, and rain can photosynthesize breathing trees to sway in the breeze. How much blood covered the lands? Their substance is the sustenance of the microbes and bacterium that feed on that once larger than life.

Chapter 3: *Below Zero: Elohim, Men of Renown

Arial, axial, bent waves, saturated—a primordial space where the dustbin collects its static debris. No one witnessed A'an striding into this sector; he came from the Celestial Empire, forged from the heart of the Sun. Scaling the back of a porpoise who swam straight to a shiny island on the Earth. His ship landed with its stern on the shores of Peru, the bow in French Polynesia.

Our mission to place the stones had begun—we started to dance and move the mighty, shiny pillars letting them rest in various positions according to their individual pitch and tonal vibration. We were obviously working with very rudimentary tools—forms from the Earth Herself.

Commissioned by the Eye of Eta Carina (himself), we set out to anchor Four Facets in a brilliant luminescent green light. We would start in the corner, which is the exact middle and work our way in an outward spiral.

Through movement and mindful articulation pitched, we fluted and weighted thoroughly each and every Facet to the turns of each new season. We worked upon each stone—laying them according to their polarity to the planet.

The Fact that Man has any Facet there at all is astonishing itself. Oh, the Galactic outcries! As if someone burned and bruised All of Creation but was invited back again to Host!

For what wrath that did occur in photon beings? It's laughable, the insult incurred upon the treacherous! They are a vying breed toying with you—killing you—emulating anything, owning nothing—not even their own will.

Therein lies the reason for all of this: man—through his own will—lived, loved, gave life, took life, created, destroyed, ascended, fell, and died. By his own hand, Man took to immortal planes in the sky. And rose. Of course, there is no rose without the thorn and that is what we are here to remove: the scales will fall from your eyes.

Oh yes, scales will fall from your Eyes!

Your blindness is not from a lack of sight. It's from a lack of vision. "Oh, and the deaf are not listening, is that what you're telling me?" you will retort. In short, yes.

Karma, reincarnation, consequence—all of these are human made constructs of our conscience? Perhaps so, yes, perhaps not, no.

◆◆◆

Cataclysms have happened on a grand scale on this particular planet (Earth) at least three times. What occurred when the dinosaurs went extinct doesn't count as a grand-enough cataclysm or catastrophe. Your present timeline—or, rather, your present perceptual perspective—doesn't allow for the permutations of multidimensional "knowing."

In other lifeforms of alternate dimensions (or even 3D), the perspective and perception is far different.

I say "or even 3D" because the consideration for all sentient 3D lifeforms is the possibility that 3D doesn't even exist but for us—at all. That is why you aren't finding other life forms out there in the cosmos—perhaps they don't exist in 3D space. 3D is bottom-rung level life and its frequency is formed for spirit-soul-body incarnation. In other words, 3D was flawed before the spirit-body-soul incarnation—3D in its entirety is flawed.

The ripple that ran through the fabric of space and time in 3D sliced it from Archernar to Deneb. But, it's not a rip so much as a place where invisible (to your eyes) light escapes from, just like the visible light of the Galactic Center is seen by your eyes, you see merely blackness when peering into the rift of invisible light.

"When we came up through the ground…"

Why do bells chime? And your Sky is our Earth. Your sky is lightning and thunder like mad pacing of the gods!

The waters rise and tidal waves collide. How much more could the land have been besieged and bereft of balance? The continents congregate and magnetize to faraway places under the Black Sun that once was.

And, the beings that lived so long that they turned to stone when the rains came, aimed towards the sky. And, on their faces etched deep into the landscape—surprise! And they then asked the heavens, "Why?"

Your once great men of renown are now merely faces in the ground.

◆◆◆

Many Giants grabbed for something—as if for protection—and obviously it did not work; whoever came into contact with surface ground would flash or turn to stone along with the hundreds of thousands of others who flashed, vaporized, burned, melted, drowned and/or petrified in and out of the rising waters.

Other Giants are still encased in ice near the poles. The ice is a great preserver of things and mimics the very activities that were happening when catastrophe struck—forever embossed onto whatever matter they stood on.

Figure 39. (Google Earth, n.d.) Petrified skull near North Pole.

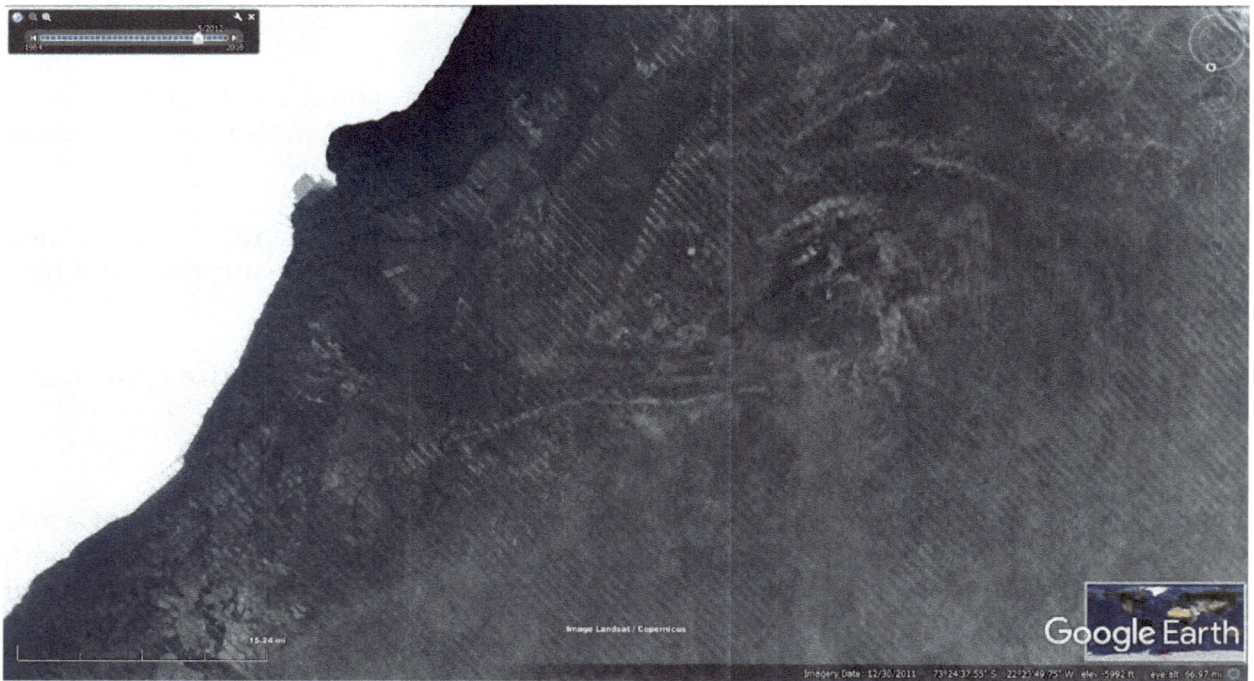

Figure 40. (Google, 2011, December 30) Clear depiction of Giants battling one another. The smaller Giant on the left is holding some kind of spear like weapon and holding the bigger Giants off in the middle to right side of the picture.

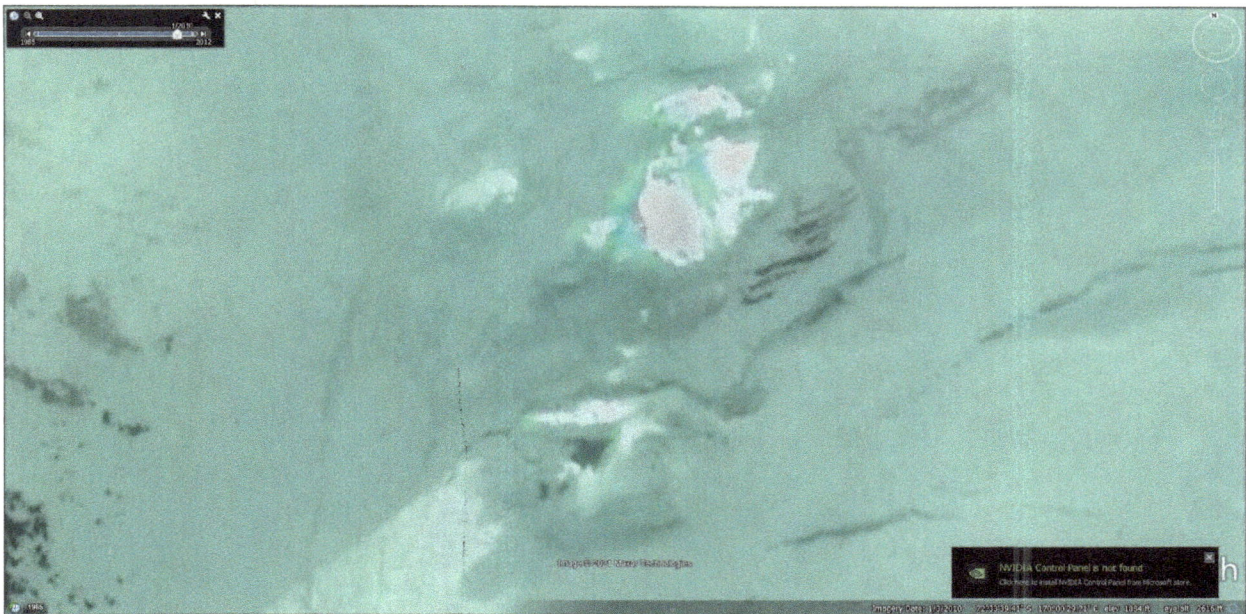

Figure 41. (Google, 2010, January 3) Face in the ice.

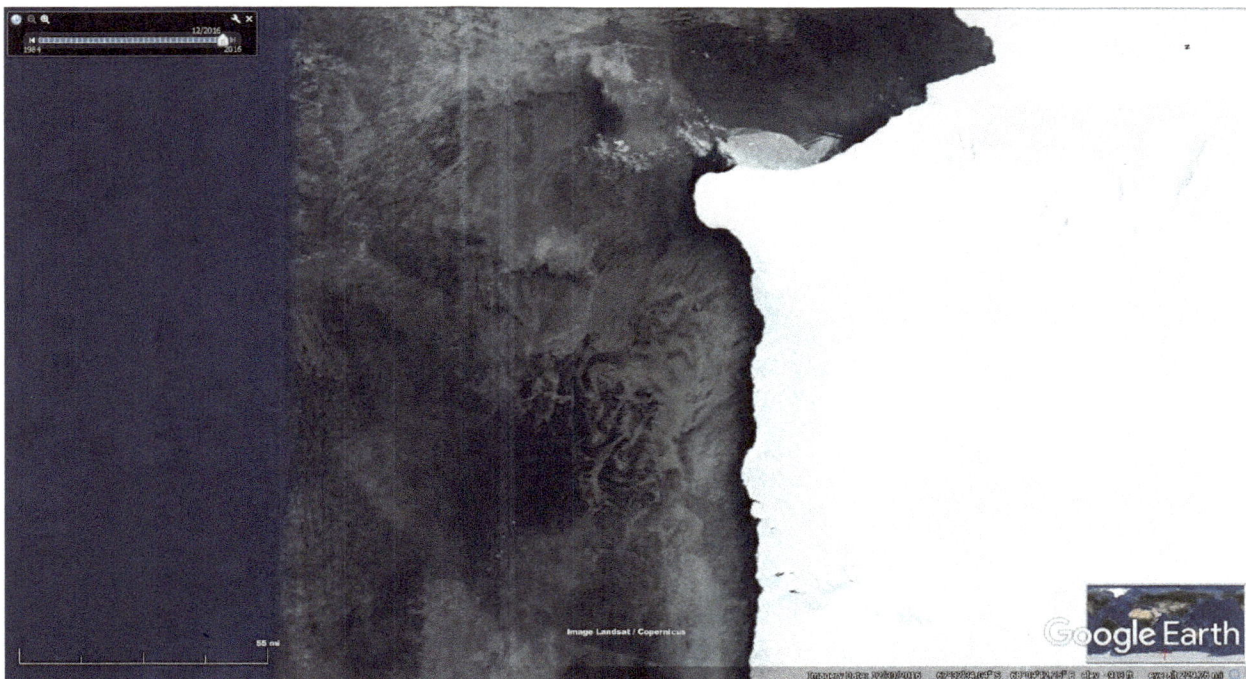

Figure 42. (Google, 2016, December 30) Hard to make out what's what but I see eyes and limbs.

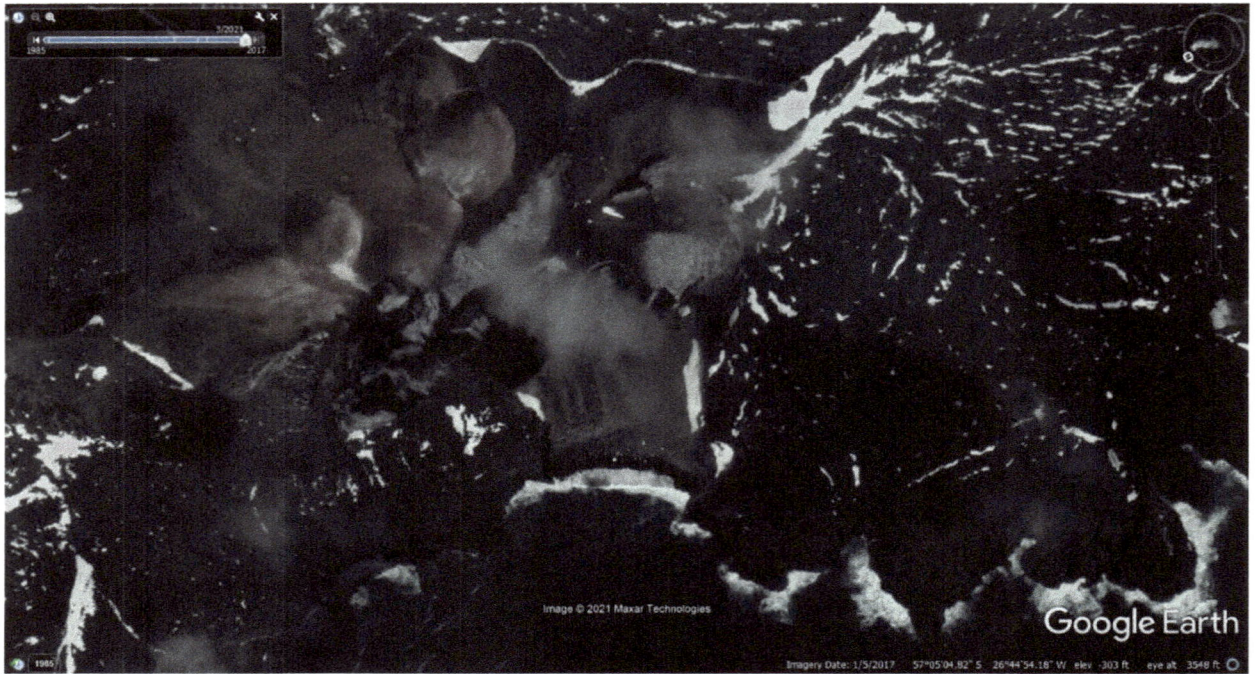

Figure 43. (Google Earth, 2017, January 5) Frowning Giant with teeth most clearly distinguished.

Figure 44. (Google Earth, 2012, October 7) Clearly, a head with the beheading hands still on it.

Figure 45. (Google, n.d.). A Giant is lying in the open palm of a much bigger Giant. Another hand is clasping the first hand from the other side.

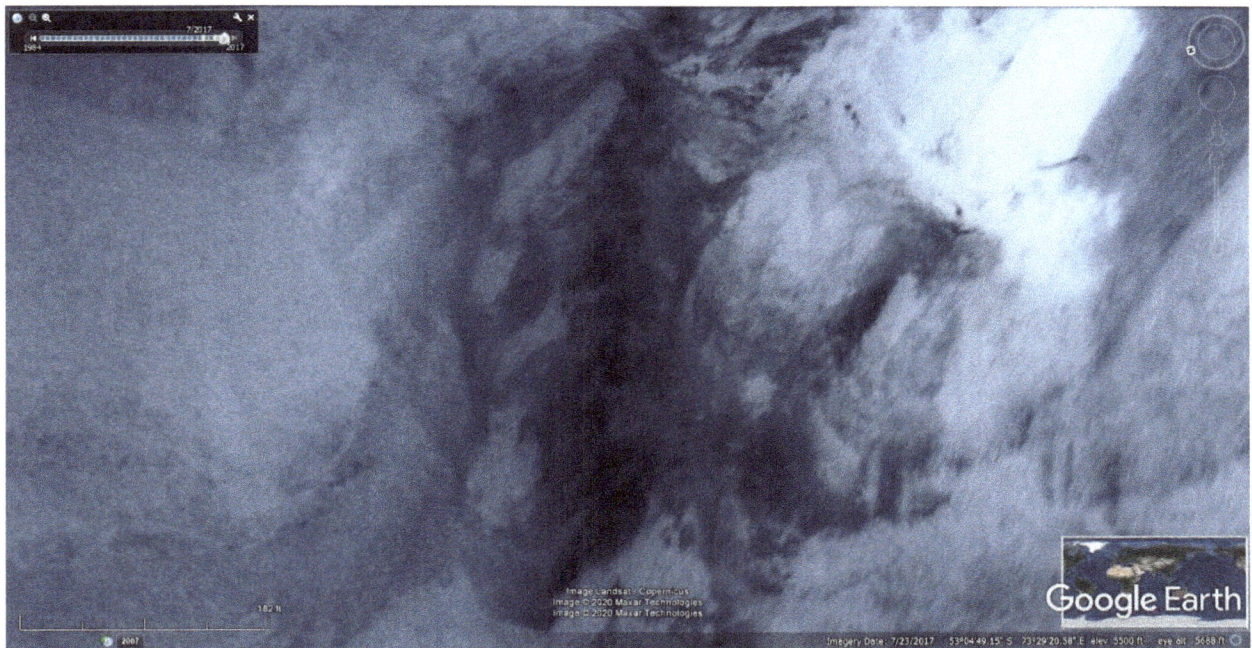

Figure 46. (Google, 2017, July 23) Two heads, one is being grabbed by a set of hands from the top corner right.

Figure 47. (Google, 2009, February 3) Head in ice.

Figure 48. (Google, 2016, December 30) Mouth agape Giant with what looks like some weapon embedded in his head.

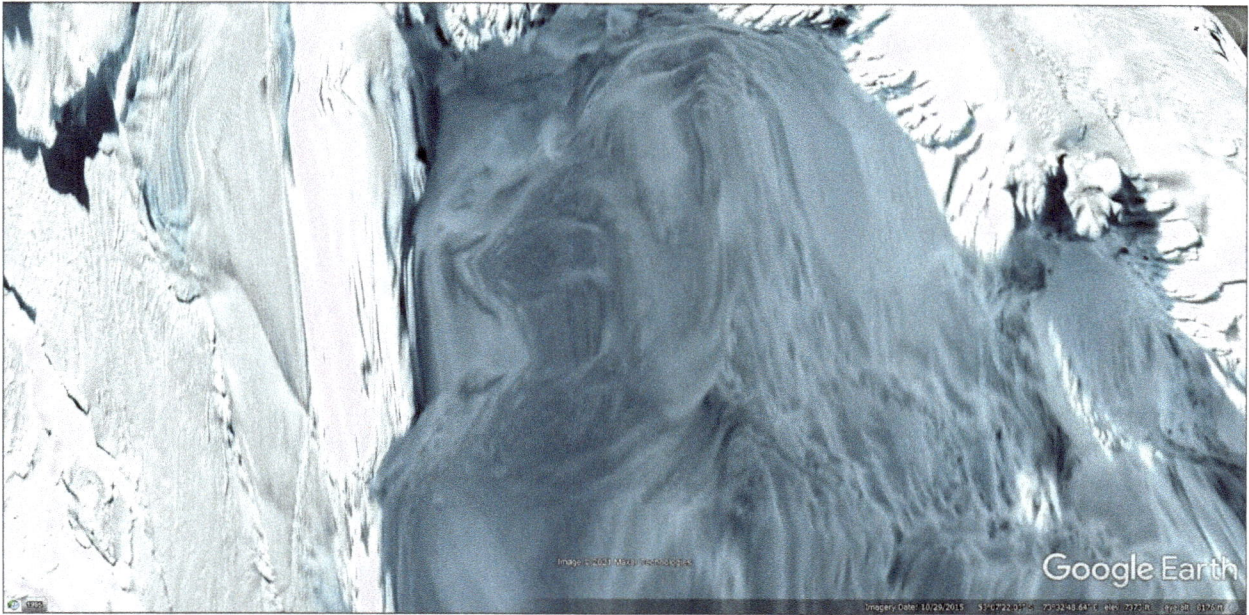

Figure 49. (Google, 2015, October 29) Gnarly-looking ice Giant with icicle sharp teeth.

Figure 50. (Google, n.d.) Female Giant frozen in the ice near the North Pole.

Figure 51. (Google, 2012, January 17) Face emerging from the ice with an apparent weapon lying next to it.

Figure 52. (Google, 2010, December 9). Agape mouth of Giant with black teeth around the perimeter.

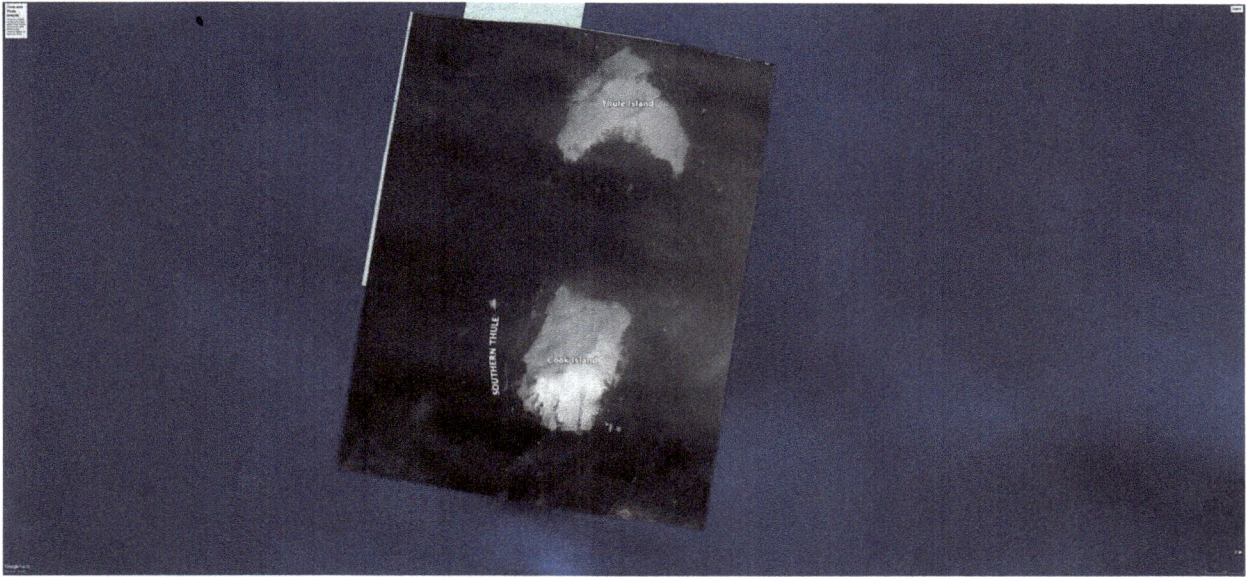

Figure 53. (Google, n.d.) Thule and Cook Islands Giants agape mouth.

Figure 54. (Google, 2012, February 5) Giant in background holding smaller Giant in forefront.

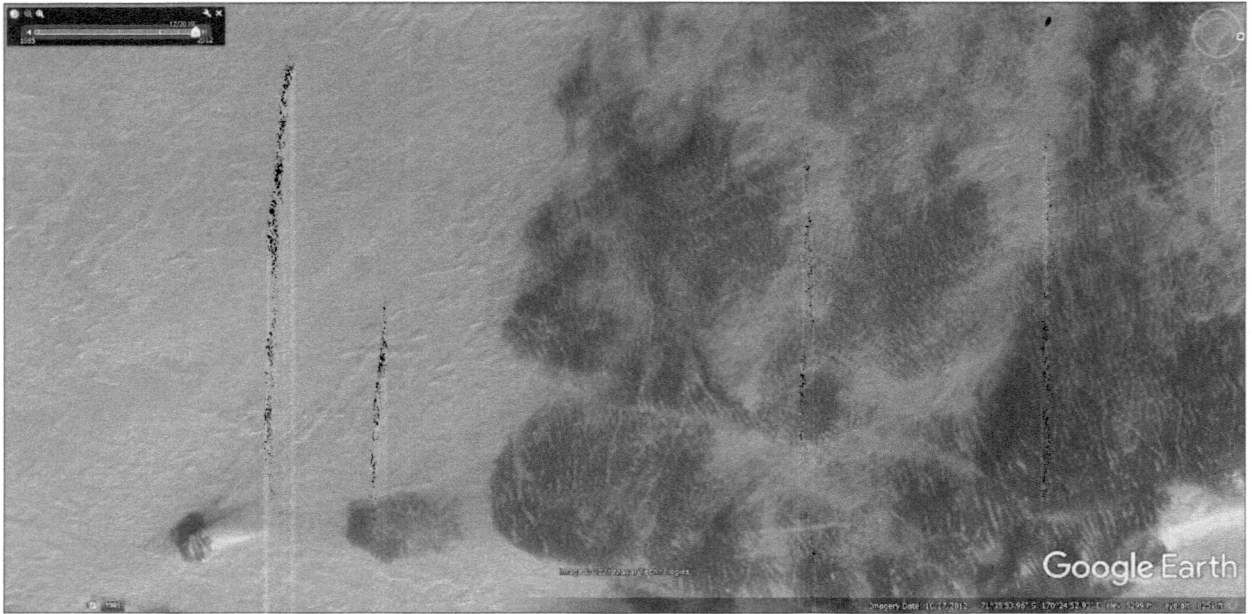

Figure 55. (Google, 2012, October 27) Profile of face.

Figure 56. (Google, 2012, October 27) Looks like a bow—bottom middle of photo.

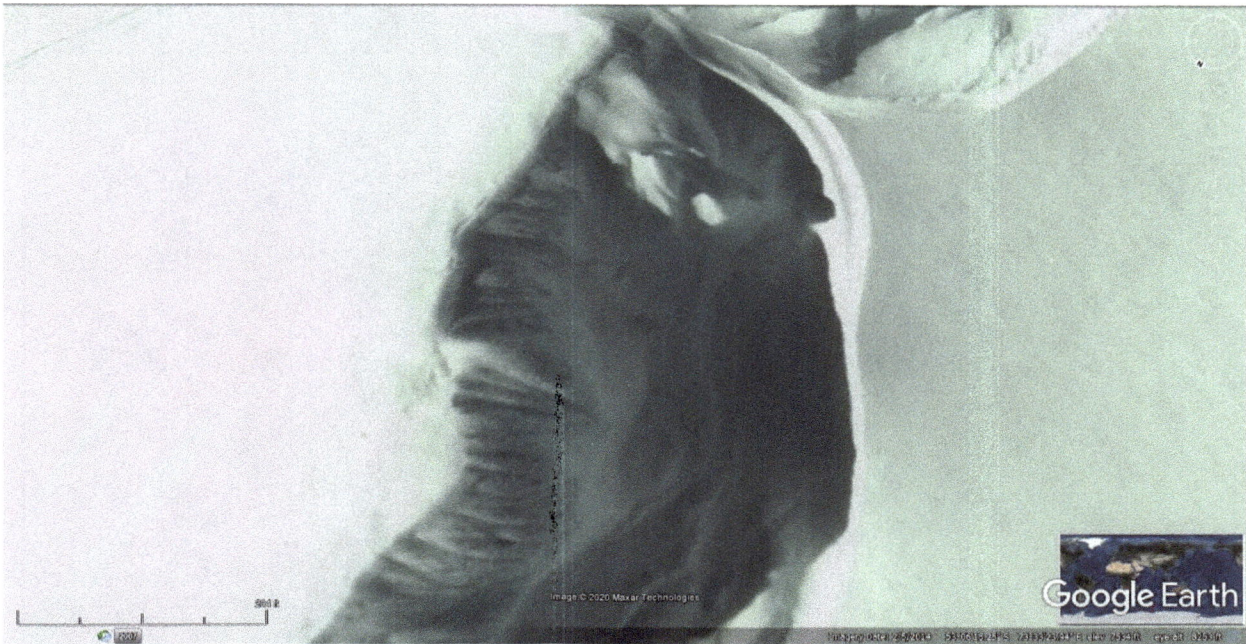

Figure 57. (Google, 2014, February 5) Another head/face emerging from snow in Antarctica.

Figure 58. (Google, 2022) Heard and McDonald Islands, one of the best examples of Giants. You can make out at least two separate Giants: arms and hands of one and the legs and backside of another.

Figure 59. (Google, 2009, February 3) Looks like a horned being; its teeth are clearly visible.

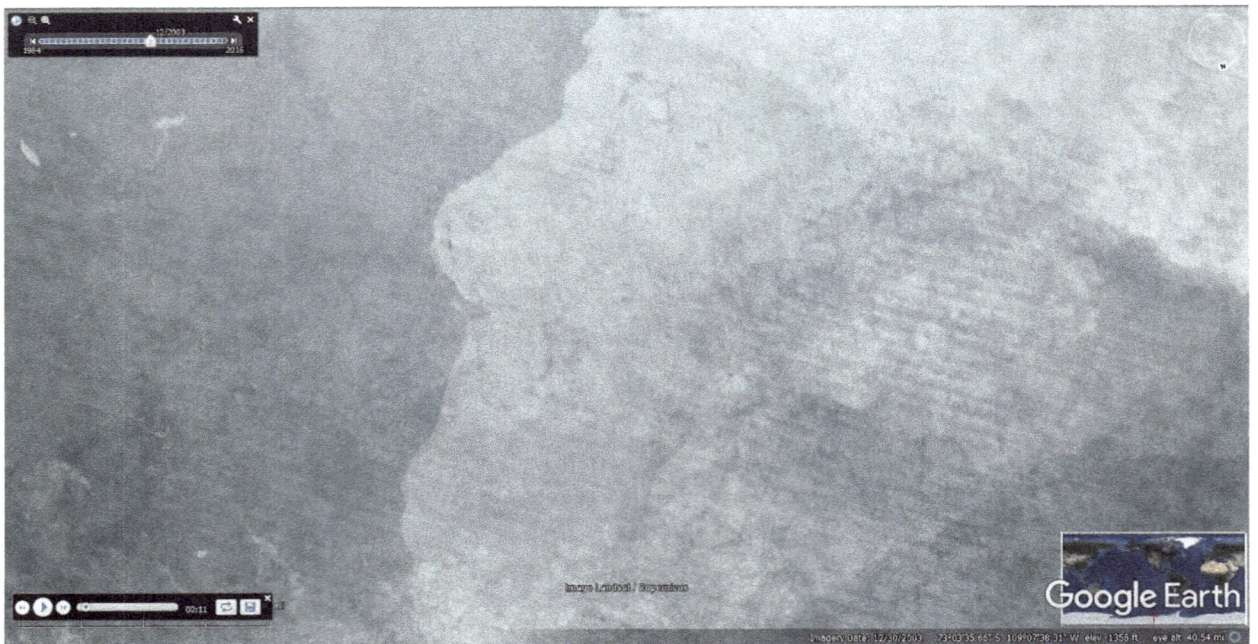

Figure 60. (Google, 2003, December 30) Head in the ice.

Figure 61. (Google, 2009, February 3) A face emerging from snow and ice.

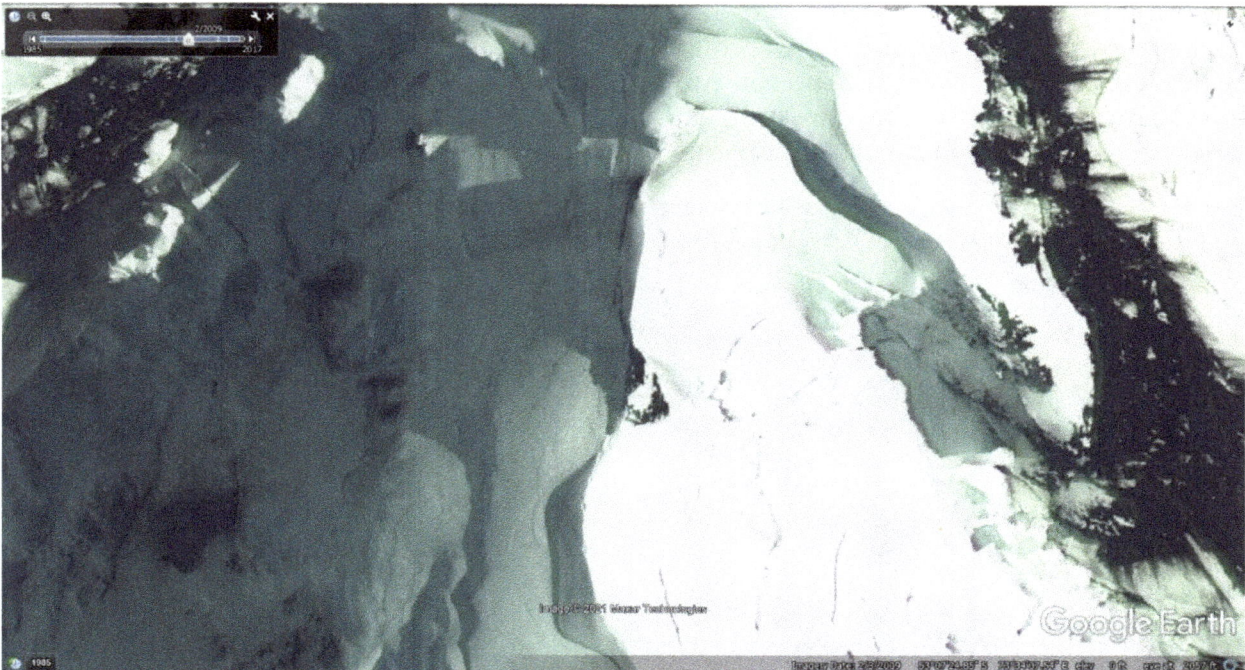

Figure 62. (Google, 2009, February 3) A Giant in the bright forefront and a face embedded in snow in the left middle.

The biggest Giants were from the time of the first cataclysm with the Titans: Marduk and Tiamat. A good lot of them are petrified leaving the bulk of their remains. In cataclysms after that some of the Giants merely vaporized(from an meteor hit or a bomb) leaving their distinctive likeness branded upon the landscape—an eerie reminder of cataclysm that to this day, our past, the curators and history writers are indoctrinated to deny and paid to hide.

And—not only their likeness once, but in two to three frames of their motions or actions— Giants are caught in the long horrific moment in mid stride. So, you have several of the same likenesses of one of those unfortunate witnesses in mid-stride imprinted on the landscape.

The Earth photographs what happens on Her; events, when they are fraught with profound emotion and at times, tragedy are impressed upon the ethers(air). What happened, apparently, a few times, was on such grand scales plus the sheer size of some of these Giants, that many of the images are still intact whether on the land, on/in ice, snow, on the water, or in the deep of the waters.

Interesting to note: It seems that the process of petrification leaves the body much smaller than when it was alive. Petrification is not unlike what happens when shrunken heads, losing all the fluid in the body results in a smaller carcass.

And: heads were coming off as if it was instructed to do so at that moment!

If you study closely the world map from the area (roughly) from Tautua through the Samoas and down even into New Zealand to the beginning of the Solomon Islands, you will see it: you can't miss it. And the Antimeridian shoots up straight through it—almost as if that giant was wielding a weapon as well as the person who got to him first. His blood is squirted from the fatal cut making up the Marshall Islands.

Figure 63. (Google, n.d.) The square object on the right of the middle is a head being decapitated.

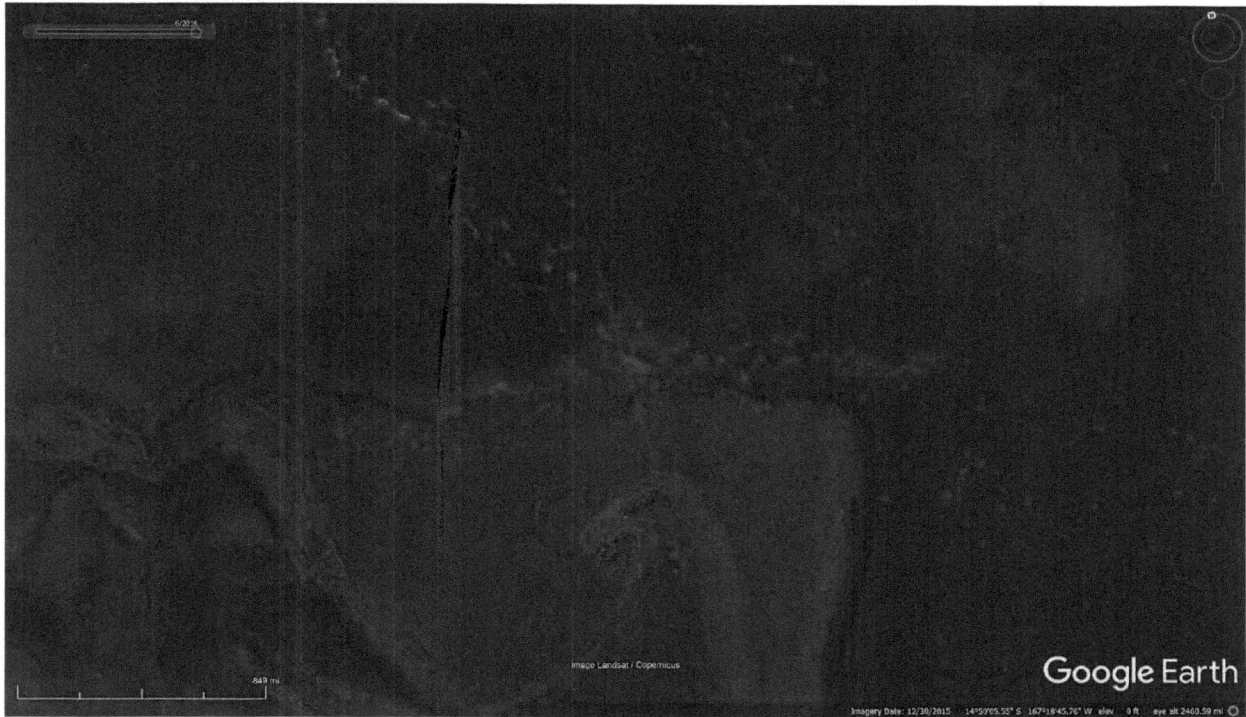

Figure 64. (Google, 2015, December 30) It is difficult to make out here but the Antemeridian runs straight up through the neck; it looks like the Antemeridian is being held in the hand of the Giant.

You see a person above another apparently wielding some guillotine whip scythe. The scenes are all over Google Earth. You have to train your eye, but it's hardly difficult. They will jump right out at you—some are so pronounced to the point of being so in-your-face that you can't *not* see it.

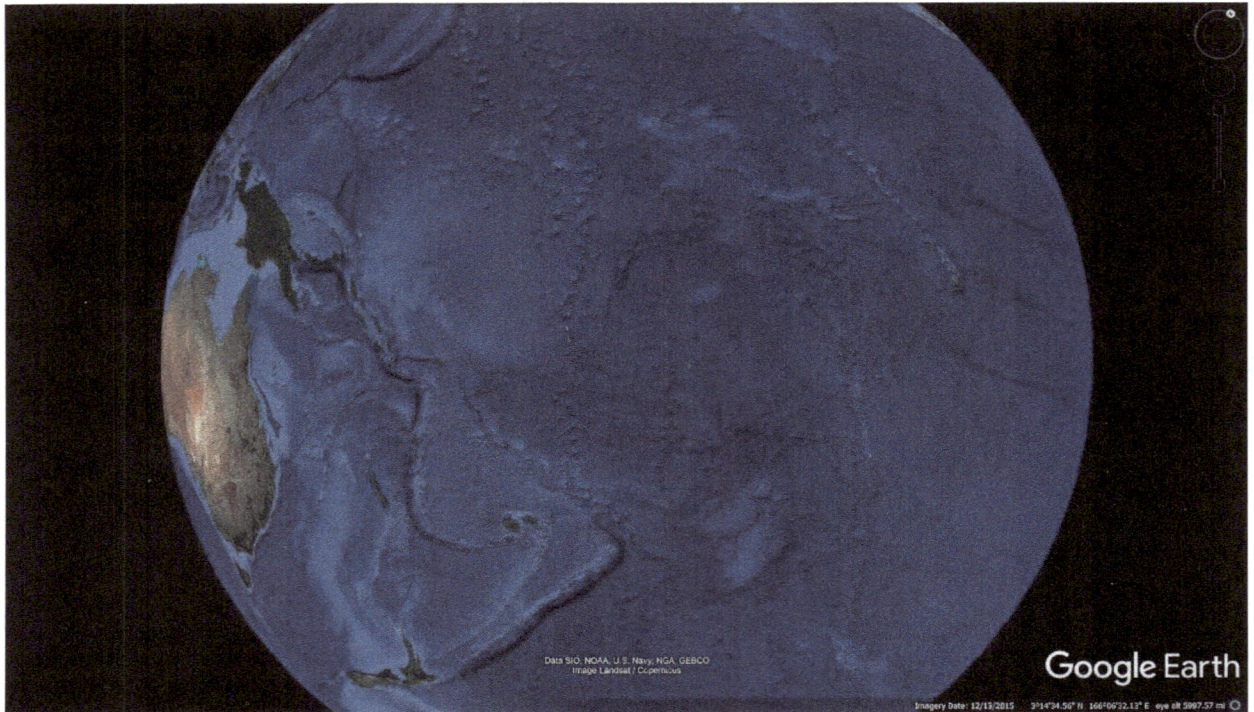

Figure 65. (Google, 2015, December 13) Larger view of area; it looks like someone is standing over a Giant and had just cut the Giant's head off. Blood and tissue from the cut make up the Marshall Islands.

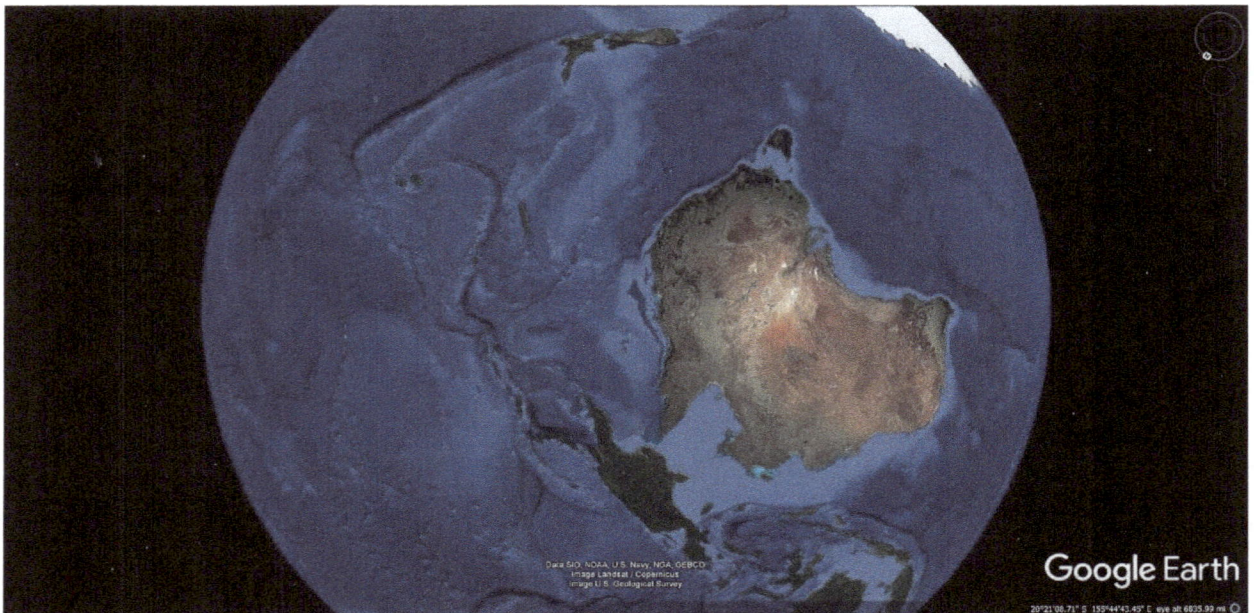

Figure 66. (Google, n.d.) A profile-to-front of a Giants face. Hair (or horn), cheekbone, nose and agape mouth clearly seen.

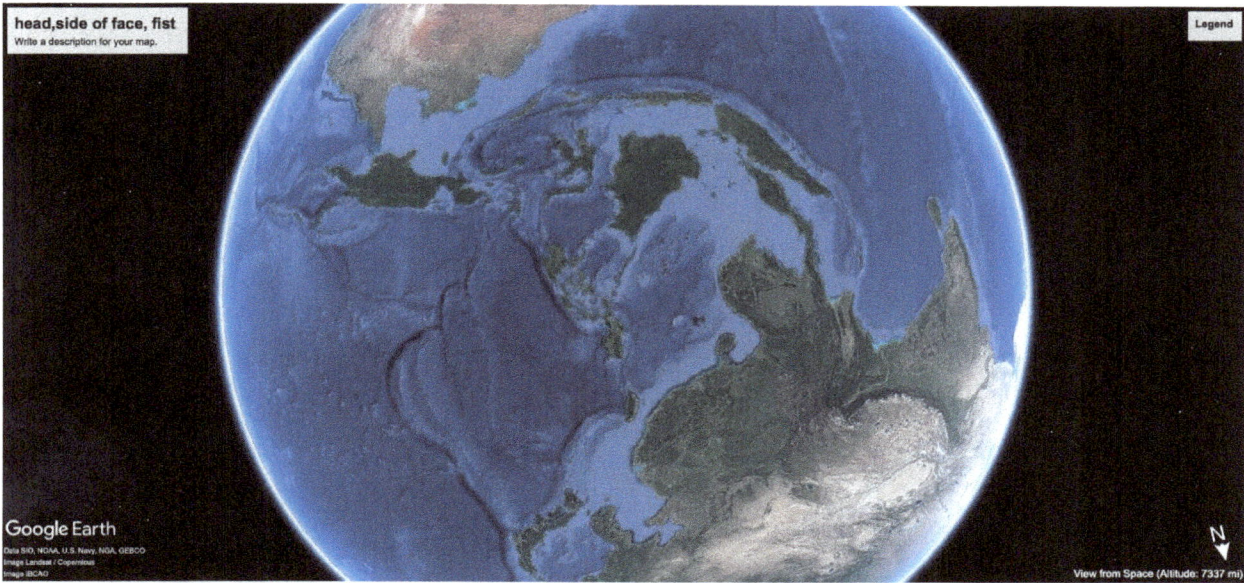

Figure 67. (Google, n.d.) Profile to back view of Giant with fist to his face

I will add that the range of size throughout the history of Giants has been planet size (and obviously much bigger in outer space) to smaller than we are now. Of course, by the time they are smaller than us, they are known as other beings: "twee folk." There appears to be all different sizes of Giants.

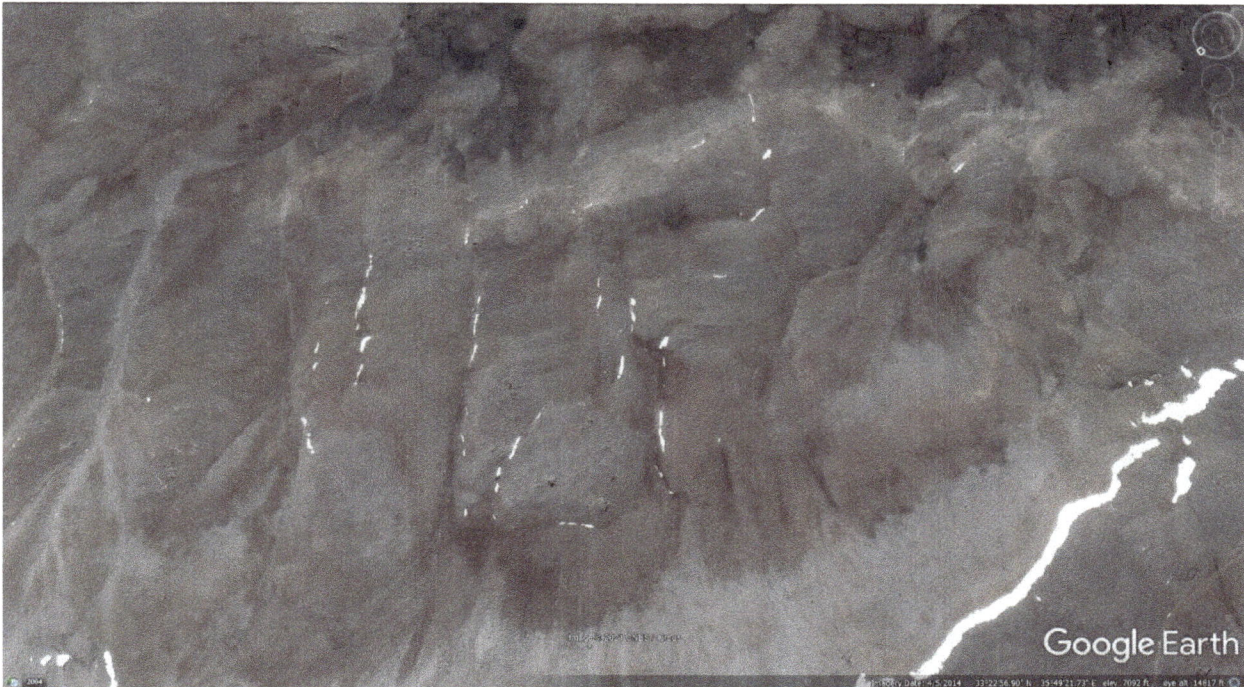

Figure 68. (Google, 2014, April 5) Heads and bodies all lined up.

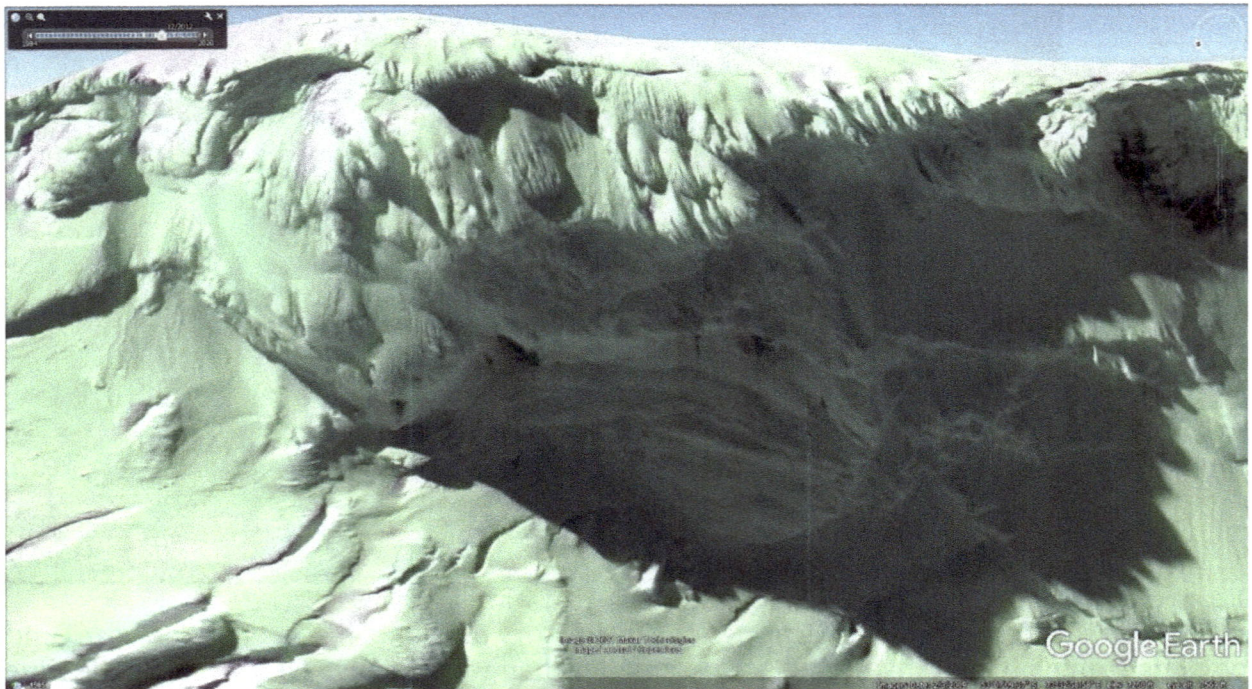

Figure 69. (Google, 2009, February 3) Partial row of teeth in center of photo. On the right side above teeth where it is smooth, looks like an ax cleave.

Figure 70. (Google, 2001) Distorted face of a Giant

Figure 71. (Google, 2009, March 29) Face melting into itself; eyes and mouth are clearly visible.

Figure 72. (Google, 2012, June 22)Burnt into the ground is a head with a second slightly smaller giant appearing to eat the eyeball of the bigger one.

In the Google Earth photos, Giants appear to be getting their heads cut off by a bigger Giant—a lot of times popped off by the bigger Giant's hand; they are also getting their genitalia cut off or ripped right from their bodies. In some cases, this is what appears to be happening.

You will find, like I said, a lot of head-chopping; you will also see many clasping hands with another to try to save them. Or, just grasping hands in general—they see what's coming so they are trying to comfort others. More hands clasping another trying to pull people out of the rising water, perhaps.

Another place to study on Google Earth is the area between the Gulf of Mexico and the Caribbean Sea. From the western side of the Caribbean Sea to the islands on the far east end of the Caribbean Sea—that huge flat looking area is from the heaving and cleaving from an ax type weapon that just cut a Giant right through the face.

Figure 73. (Google, n.d.) One can see the top of the head of a Giant from the bottom of Belize to the bottom of Cuba to the top of Cuba; the huge area looks like a bell-The upper Gulf of Mexico. This Giant was cleaved right through the face. His teeth are on the other side of the ax cleave in the Atlantic and make up that chain of Islands from the British Virgin Islands to Aruba. Another head is on the other side of Panama—in the Pacific ocean and includes the Galapagos Islands. The headless body floating away from the second head's mouth indicates the second bigger giant was eating the third and smallest one.

The frozen ice on Antarctica is melting faster than the powers that be are able to conceal the bodies of Giants thawing and strewn across the landscape. Giants will be exposed and open with no way for Google Earth to conceal without raising suspicion.

My guess is that is why Google is phasing out the software program and putting Google Earth on the browser. I'm certain that they will do away with the software program—period. I'm sure they have known for years and years that the ice was uncovering Giants; they probably figured it wouldn't be melting so fast.

And, the slow phasing out of the clarity of objects in pictures on Google Earth is something they've—I'm sure—have had in place since the program first had public access. Too many questionable looking objects!

Much of the time, however, Giants will have had their heads actually popped off by even bigger Giants. You can't look at Google Earth without seeing these horrific scenes but you have to know what you're really looking at.

Often, zeroing in on a place will indicate a particular scene but, until you pull back a bit and separate the bodies (and see things as they appeared to have happened), you won't understand what you are seeing!

The same thing can be said about he who breaks out of Her. He blew his icy wind that froze the poles as he wielded a whip scythe. As the breastplate was snatched from Her general and he was thus lain slain, the breastplate has sat under ice in Greenland since before Pangea.

I'm no forensics expert, but—depending on the position of the body at death—things may not always stay to decompose where the Giant died. I see eyeballs that don't stay in place in the sockets—sometimes, they will roll away from the body and other such features.

The place where a Giant's corpse ended up after waters receded also depends on the rate of decomposition and other factors especially water or sunlight and whatever insects or animals are feeding on the body.

Across the Earth, you will see many Giants in mid-scream at what's happening around them: faces turned skyward, mouths agape and stretched to ridiculous lengths. This happened much more than one can even imagine.

The entire Eastern coast of North America is made of a Giant whose agape mouth stretches from the middle of Georgia, Alabama and Mississippi all the way up to upstate New York. If you flip your map upside down on Google Earth, you can see it.

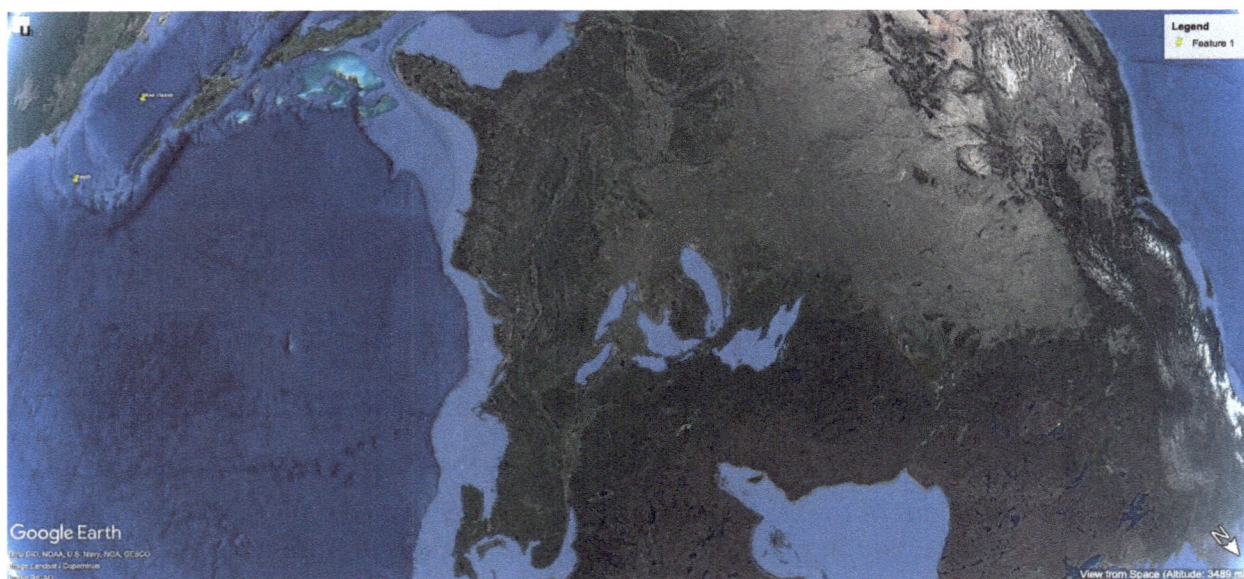

Figure 74. (Google, n.d.) Most of the eastern United States is taken up by a humongous open mouth. You can see up into the nostrils (southern US) and also the tongue sticking out over and in between Lake Erie and Lake Ontario.

Figure 75. (Google, n.d.) Huge hand with visible fingers and thumb reaching down from Alaska, Canada, Washington, Oregon and extending into all of California, Arizona, New Mexico, Nevada and Utah. The hand is holding something, either another hand or a smaller Giant.

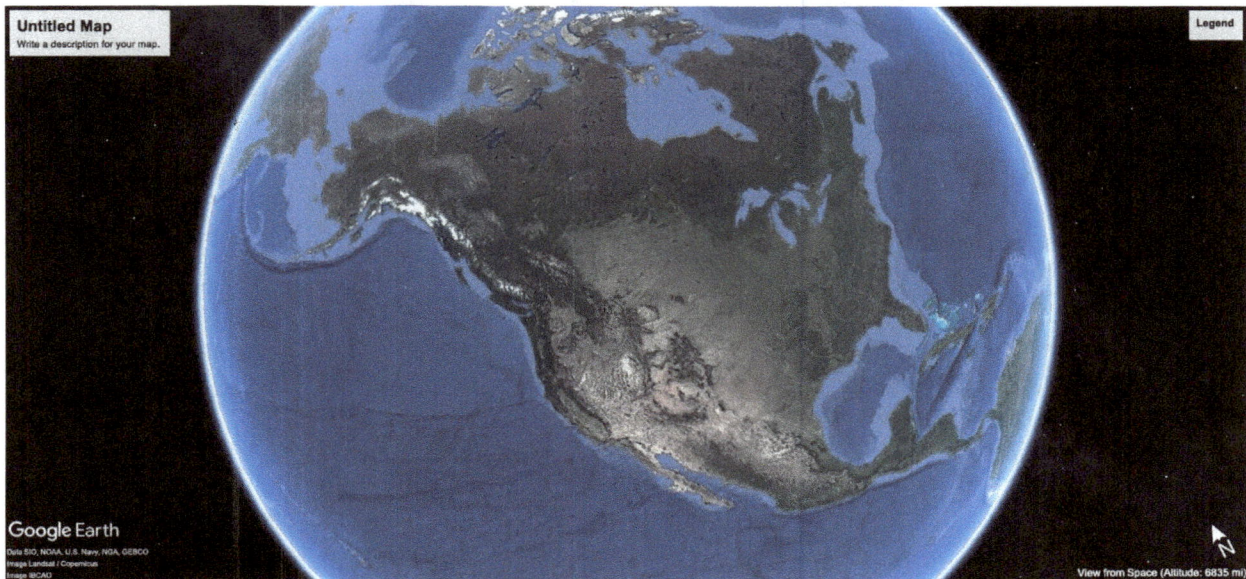

Figure 76. (Google, n.d.) Huge Giant with legs apart, one leg running along the western US, the other (or the leg is from another Giant) torn off and running up under another Giant's mouth into Maine into Canada(leg and foot). Crotch is the red area in the southwest US. The anus is the Inland Empire to the Salton Sea in Southern California into Mexico. The chest is upper Canada; stomach lower Canada. The Giant is headless with its head in upper Canada next to Alaska.

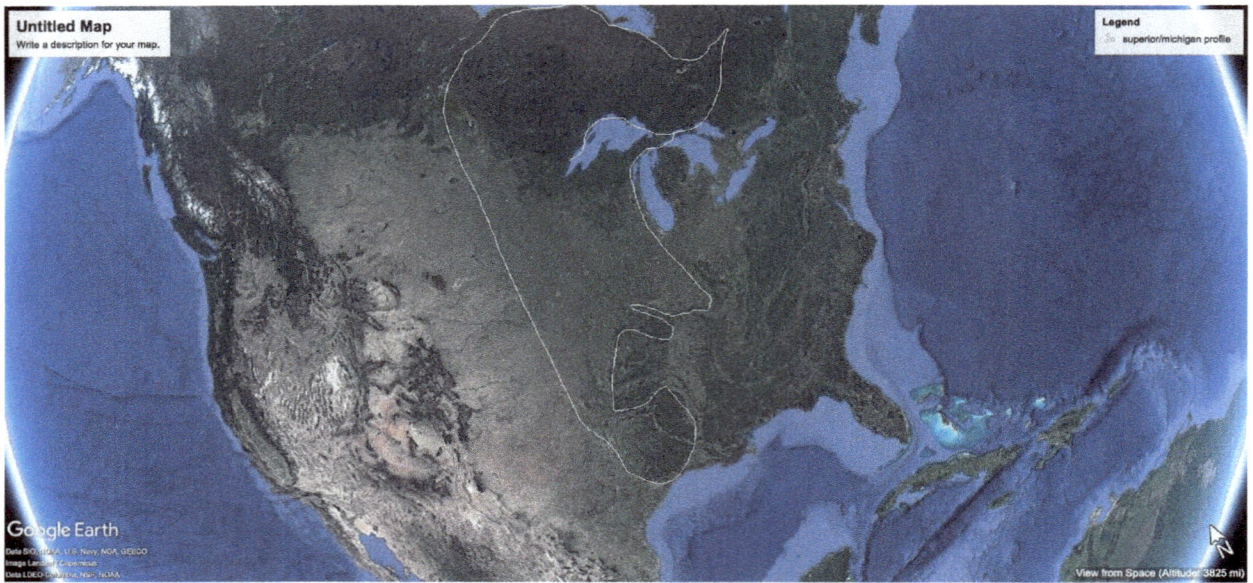

Figure 77. (Google, n.d.) To give an idea of what to look for, the profile of a Giant extending throughout a good portion of the Midwest and well into Canada.

Figure 78. (Google, n.d.) See above caption of Figure 77.

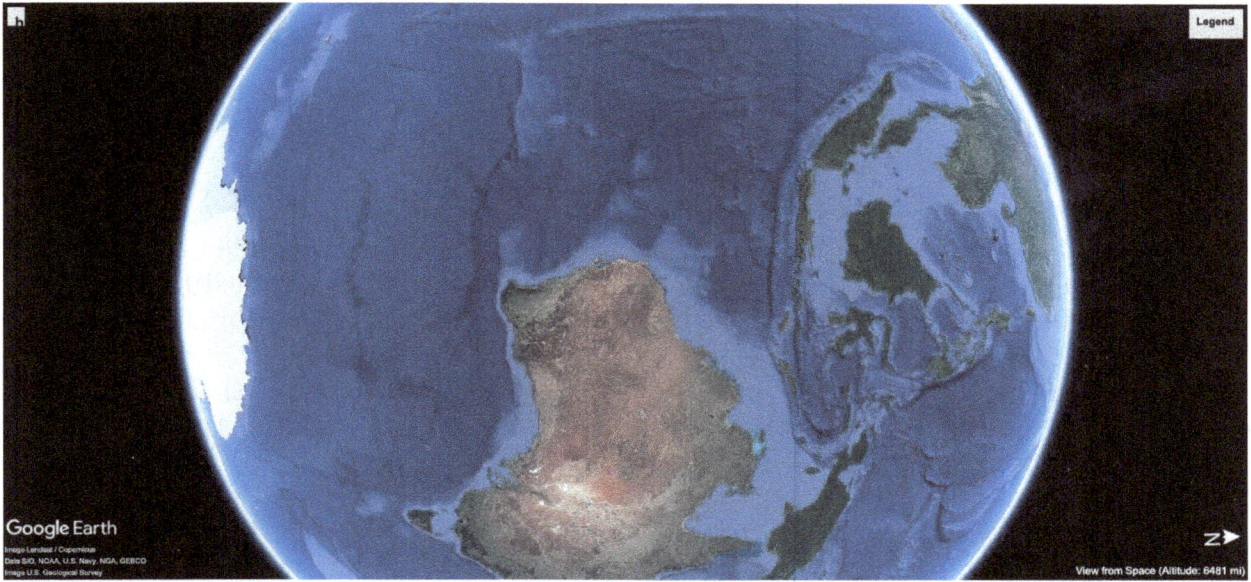

Figure 79. (Google, n.d.) Weapon-wielding Giant, arm above his head striking a blow or it could be a gigantic head facing left, eye sockets in the ocean, open mouth roughly from Balladonia to Yellabina and the Great Australian Bight (hmm...).

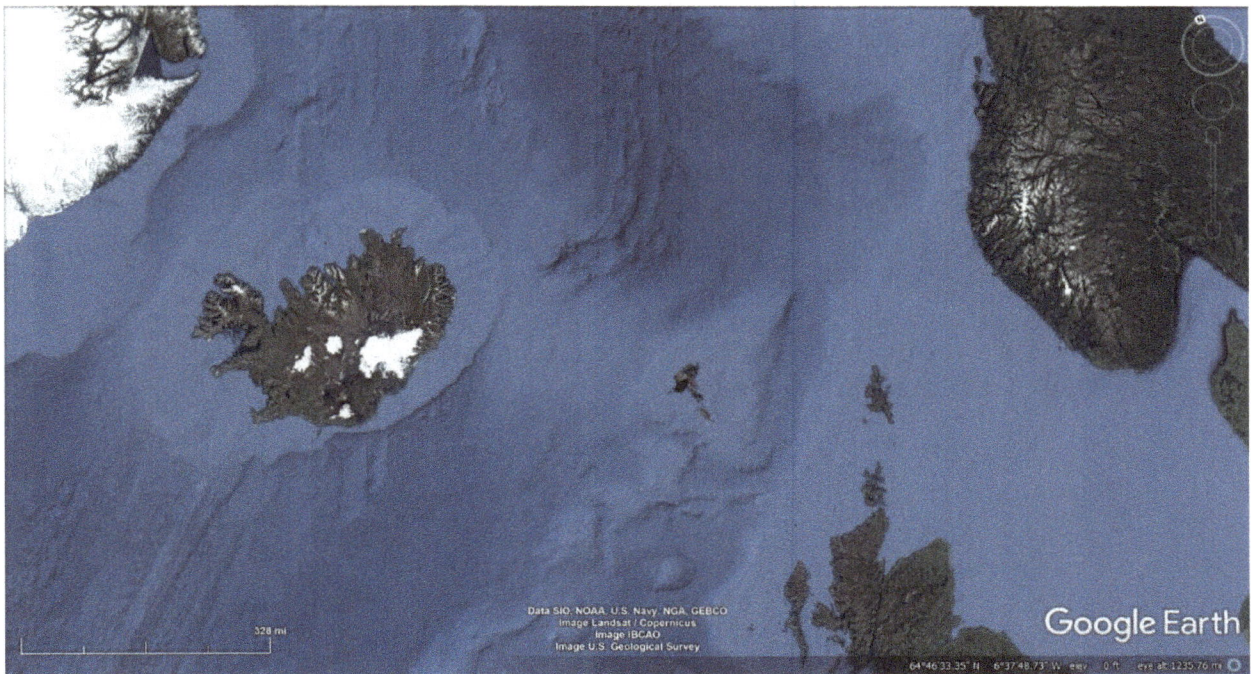

Figure 80. (Google, n.d.) Eye, broken nose, mouth clearly visible.

Chapter 4: *Sea Level: The Toroid Earth

Yes, the Earth was larger in those days—She was. Giving birth to dancing Stars, the original O.G. Chao(s). Before her last general was torn from her and made into the Moon. Days and Nights as Tia Maat under Mardukkian siege and reign. Is he not still within Her? Did he not raise the fever and pitch, until no more could She catch Her breath?

When he breathed fire ice winds, it seized Her up and She flashed brittle and the water displaced. To freeze in that rich cold environment...let's just say your poles preserve better than any cryogenics.

Care to be taken when you dare to awaken the sleeping Giant who just may be your shadow. How many times have you been here before? How many millions of lives have you endured and every time see the same faces, wars, and constructs? And, written in the Stars, you must commence to be upon that still purple soft dirt and take up thy home.

But, like all slaves made dumb by divine birthright by being severed from our internal life, we are causing fragmentation and death to the host body but not the indwelling meshed soul and over spirit.

We were supposed to overcome in order to raise our vibrations and change our frequency, especially of our physical bodies. And finally, it looks as though that can really happen. Ah, there was a glimmer among you! In fact many of you—if you could just find each other! Critical mass x light exponential = skipping a few levels. And without the mass trauma to achieve it!

Else the Four Facets—our toil—would lay to waste. We would not have been broached to contract. We do know certain Futures.

We could very well be autonomous, at last—until then we can only dream of being intergalactic ambassadors.

This planet is still in a state of decomposition with many monsters dead and they are still tethered to Her as She lives on. Catching Her breath, she presses on with serpentine magnetism, winds into and out of Her torrid-like ebb and flow—pulsing and rhythmic, yes flames leaping into one another.

"Do you remember me?"

You see, he merely scalped Her—Her head is quite intact(ed). But She'll do Her best to make you think She has lost it! And, had you read the report...but of course you couldn't! That bit was redacted.

And, She'll live again and again until all memories are reenacted. Even though She is the arche-prototype and Sorghum was made from Her brow. Her first brow-born baby of thought manifested, birth pangs swelled up the night, blocking the very eclipsed black sun. In the midst of eclipse from the heart of the Sun came the dance of Creation and was flung to the outermost regions-among the Starry arms of Albion.

Distant sisters looked to their eighth one in this direction—don't you see the resemblance? This planet is in the Bull's Eye of Sacred Chao. At once, the seventh in and third out—then juxtapose the two. Which makes the third and seventh one like Nut, taken to the Sky?

> Worlds are made from spin, around and around like cotton candy
> Daisies know they have a sun to grow and they have no want to desire
> A Moon of Maldek—Mars—scorched, scarred and sandy Dog Days and Dragon
> Nights—beyond Alcyon, what is higher?

See: the brightness upon awakening and dance in the fire light! Eclipse of the Black Sun—Saturn—in the time before the White Sun: Sol.

Losing sight of the task at hand is this planet's biggest obstacle. Nearly everyone has forgotten. No one remembers why they are here. To take what you are currently doing in your life, ask yourself: "Is this what I imagined? Is this what I pictured would be when I fell into Earth's gravity?" If so, you are fortunate and one of the few!

Full conscious and aware sentient presence is necessary for self-realization; it's not something you can buy, sell, give, trade, or have someone else do for you. It is like so many things; it grows within you. And you can take it to heart or tear it apart.

Do you know why you are here?

He's breaking out of Her to the North! You can still see his face as he blew over what became the North Pole. Titans confronted by Monsters in turn made to stand at each station.

Shall I mention? Each one in his own turn! Each one a different dimensional door: the one we view in this time/space continuum is in Virgo, as She is giving birth. And you are beholden to the golden Regulus not far from this. Is he to sire your good Fortune?

In All of the celestial empires forged in the heart of the sun, could you retrieve it or even believe your paradise had barely begun?

Wayward whistles the wind and wonders when? And then he's begotten again!

As seen from Venus, a conjunction lining up Maldek and Mars—at that time a moon of Maldek—the Black Sun (Saturn), Earth and opposing Pluto, Uranus and the yet to be the sun Sol, and well, several ages were no more.

For an incredibly long amount of time—the height, width, depth, and distance of time since the beginning, a tear ripped everything sideways and upset more than just Creation. Apparently, the crack goes down the entire length of the Universe. (Although it does appear from your perspective on Earth the tear could be that 90 degree blind spot at the edge of peripheral sight that merely casts shadows over making it appear torn.)

Earth has many scars in the form of giants eroded into the terrain and Venus has as well . The rate of decomposition of Venus' Giants is a bit different as they are less visible and the remains from those giants are slow-baked in a high carbon dioxide environment.

Before the Maldek cataclysm, Venus was more like Earth and hosted a large Giant population and was prolifically green. Venus' atmosphere was not so dense but the planet was. With that cataclysm, the Giants died—most life forms perished. Venus flashed with intense heat just long enough to cause the water in it to come to the surface, causing condensation in the atmosphere but not enough heat to heat up the ground and giving it the heavy cloud layer that we see today.

◆◆◆

The slash of his whip sliced the entire length of the universe. His Heaven is your Earth and avalanches tumble down hard. The landscape was covered with destruction, death, and untimely upheaval. No one waited to listen—hungry he was to take his crown. North, North winds carry the cry.

Like sirens in the ice, the banshees of the northwest and the monsoons of the southeast, forever echoing in screeches and groans. At once, She startles and listens, and elicits in an instant the position to hold on to some land from Murmanskin (I can't make this stuff up!) all the way down to Mandel and Hasselholm.

The length and the breadth of that land is why Marduck never had children. He couldn't. She never sounded like that before nor since, the beginnings and endings of the sweet emanations of Ain Sof.

Chapter 5: *Smog Gets in My Eyes: What Dreams are These?

We need to awaken—let the sleep fall from our eyes! Time has come for all to be known, all to be free, all to be shown! The timing is perfect from our point of view because, soon, it will be too late to change the directive.

Our complacency is despicable and, yet, we'll all go on and on like nothing is wrong, show ourselves to be dispensable. We see what is reprehensible and deny it knowingly—giving excuse to our precious life that we cling to our creature comforts only wholly.

The hoarding global elite of our time: all-consuming black vortices, continuously hoarding money, property and anything deemed valuable, squandering resources, invading countries, killing cultures full of people, tearing at the fabric that weaves the stars, tainting the very clay that molds man, rendering the space stained and hollow. The empty pitcher to be certain. They tampered with the water within; they changed the conduits' properties, altered the natural flow of the seeding, blossoming function of sowing and reaping. They break down any link to the internal dialogue of our own voices. They splintered our family units so that there is a constant and repeated disconnect between the internal and external of every being both within ourselves and with one another.

They've denied us peace, solace, the wisdom in knowledge, the ability to know instinctively and intuitively what next to do, severed the sacred link to our multidimensional perception, clouded and shrouded our purpose, led us to want valueless things in excess. They caused cognitive dissonance and sapped our soul. It made the light a lie so that nothing is what it looks like because we can be what we want in the dark.

The collective consciousness of All suffers an arrhythmia in the soul—as you can see in our lights as they blink and flicker. The environmental toxicity of our present world will not yield a healthy crop or even a true one with all the seed genome tampering with our deadliest pesticides. In the grand scheme of things, this is a huge issue but so is everything else the powers that be do of the vilest, sickest, most twisted form of allegiance with evil forces to deprave the human soul and destroy the human spirit.

Reptilians to archons to other shape shifting beings who run the world work on a very emotional and mental plane somewhere between the lower 3rd to 5th dimensions. They are able to shift and move about largely unnoticed as to what they are by the undiscerning eye. But, those who are able to see light within light and the shadows they cast within them, they instantly recognize these vying, heart-reversed creatures.

These beings resemble wretched, pleading demons ever starved for blood, ego, objects, feeling, land, space, control, money, power, and adulation. Their assimilation is to the lowest and crudest desires of a vacant conscience, ***to see other living things as objects that will bend to their will.***

Their desire for control is hardly the product of altruistic intent. Money is not the only thing that separates philanthropy from humanitarianism. Their generosity is duplicitous, still serving themselves somehow so that they get all the advantages of being a benefactor with none of the pure and present heart-connected empathy and compassion it takes to actually be one. (Side-note: Empathy is not necessarily compassion. I've met lots of Empaths who have no compassion and, of course, the opposite is true, as well).

They move in and among their own self-serving circles, helping only those who serve to further their agenda. They do things under the guise of "doing us a good deed" (as a guilt trip) when it is in fact detrimental in every way possible way but now we've been brainwashed by "everything is okey-dokey"—but we are really just a way to keep rein on what or who they want to control. In other words, they weren't going out of their way to "do us a good deed." And now they are busy being scurrilous telling others how you are now "taking advantage" of their generosity. Heavy strings attached. Payment of a thing often requires no money changing hands, just your time, your attention, your blood and sweat, your stress and your eventual breakdown for *their plan for your life*. And then on top of that because they've used your name or credit now you are ruined.

They've used us to further their own agenda and keep control of the situation and now you are basically stuck—oh and by the way—it only appears to others or they've failed at convincing us of their falsely pure motives that they've done for us this act of altruism.

All the while with this hocus-pocus over here, they will completely abandon other responsibilities (foisted upon still others) over there. Doesn't matter how nice and polite our exchange of words is with them—the messages are in the actions alone and they speak volumes. Especially if now their actions directly affect what we do or don't do—what we can or cannot do.

They boast bravado about pebbles to stone next to our visions of semi-precious gems that we wouldn't mind sharing one bit if it weren't for the blatant disrespect for us as individuals and them placing us below their own lowly position—which they've no doubt usurped to begin with. These people are opportunists for the benefit of those who conspire with them.

They default on their words constantly—promise it all now only to feign ignorance of such an agreement later. They attempt to masterfully convince us and themselves of their "purity" often by virtue signaling themselves on the first face while "warning" us of an enemy we've never met on the second face.

They do not believe in true distribution—they may offer you a job, for instance, and when you get yourself in a position to do that they will snag it out from under you and still expect you to break your back for zilch—while they are up your ass about your method of operation.

They are clannish, narcissistic, and show the ice in their veins by their cavalier and maudlin concern of others' well being. And right under their very noses! Their compassion is nonexistent. The pains and sufferings of others don't affect them and they act accordingly.

They will appropriate your time, your efforts, your energy to their whim all the while dictating to you how to do what they won't do themselves.

There are, of course, exceptions to this rule but I'm not talking about a special circumstance case scenario.
Adept at wrecking your flow—psychic subjugation and denial is at the deepest levels—they seem to get their kicks by interfering and throwing things out of balance. Flow Wreckers hate human progress, innovation, and our creative functions because without sublimation, creativity stagnates and becomes negative feelings that would be fed on by these psychic vampires.

And, in the end they will say that the devil made them do it. It's "do what thou wilt" when the purpose serves but, yet, they will claim ignorance of the willpower to be truly self-governing or even be a present, cognizant representative of their own soul-matrix or temple.

Instead, they employ everything from the pharmaceutical industry with its plethora of psychiatric pills to the bad timing of the highly internal process from arcane Atlantis that is "Merkaba Mechanics" to scalar wave and beast technology and V2K to control the masses.

HAARP to wreck the frequency of living things, CERN to warp the atomic structures—both irreversibly damaging DNA/RNA of every living thing. When that ULO waves to you, just say hello. ;)

The monetization of absolutely everything is already in order: taxing you from the moment you first draw breath in, the air is soon to be measured and doled out as well.

It's important to note that **All of the earthly, tangible hardware is going software—humans included**. If it's in the mind of the writer already, then it's surely within the capabilities of the elite to hire the brains to build anything imaginable. Albeit increasingly virtual.

That said, it is no surprise that deep underground military bases are incidentally made many times from the remnants of ancient giants and are built as they tunnel into the planet. They are actively hollowing Her out; it would make sense to utilize giants as underground dwelling. Some of these Giants are so big that the empty spaces inside the body in between organs or cells even would themselves be enormous.

Keep in mind that Giants had much less density to their bodies: the spaces inside of the being would be enormous by our minuscule standards. It's a no-brainer that the military would make use of these petrified, crystallized remains.

The mountains all over Earth are layered with deceased Giants—many times they died and ended up in heaps, piles of Giants swirling in rushing waters taking the bodies hither and yon, ending up piled upon each other and decomposing right there. But even then they still moved about post mortem because of the floods.

Decomposition came and saw the Giants scattered of their parts downstream and collected in various pools of similar parts from other bodies in big Giant soup sludges. Other areas where Giants were trapped in thick sticky mud and clay with one or both feet, died standing upright only to later or sooner come crashing down or simply crumpling, folding down to the ground.

This largely depended on if their ankles snapped at death because their weights wouldn't hold them once they died—they toppled over snapping at the ankles. This is an idea that to my knowledge was first introduced by Roger Spurr of Mudfossils University.

◆◆◆

It will come to exacting measures: the manner in which your children are allowed to be born and with what designer features. If they are allowed to be born at all.

No one signed up for this "pay to live, live to pay" society, where one is bought and sold from birth and herded onto the edge of a cliff like lemmings(yes I realize lemmings don't really hurl themselves over cliffs. Thanks Disney) with the constant threat of having to "perform" and outwit their peers.

Giving a good face to the world but, on the inside, knowing it's all a lie: the money, the active abolishment of human rights, the need to have control over others or to be controlled by way of conformity or some wayward, deluded idea of what a leader is supposed to be.

But, why does anyone want to be led in the first place? Do we not have the wherewithal to be self-governing? The conscience? The moral fiber? The restraint?

Can people place their faith upon the Universe or God, whoever they call their "Higher Power" to provide their needs on a day to day, minute to minute basis?

Strength in numbers does not matter when our goal is not a unified, conscious, and collective decision.

Peoples' sense of self-preservation is the one instinct they will resort to only when their actual physical space is threatened. Perhaps the problem—if you want to call it that—in America, anyway, is that no one has had their own imminent space threatened.

In our United States of America—the place where 400 years ago people fled to because of religious and political persecution only to have slaves, under a hypocrisy that stated "all men are created equal" (except here, here, and here). If the oppression doesn't kill you, the hypocrisy will! And the denial is so deep that it's not even considered by the perpetrators—it's not just a river in Egypt.

Oppression itself is repressed, much of it in the shadows, underlying the ominous at every turn while our freedoms have long begun to be eliminated. Our governments worldwide have been infiltrated and taken over by capitalistic psychopaths whose megalomania (approaching that of the demiurge) means they will just soon depopulate the world quickly (and get everyone's platinum) so they can divvy up the planet among themselves.

However, even if it had gone that far, since there is no honor among thieves, the planet's resources never would have been equally distributed and in the final etheric record, no such thing ever even came close.

Not that their plans were flawed in-and-of-themselves; it's that their loyalties are perverse, their intentions reversed—they are not forward spinning wheels and their cogs are clogged with the metallic run-off that is the dross of their soul and ever diminishing spirit and ability to feel.

Repeated histories of violence, trauma, pain, subjugation continue to grip the masses as we buy into the official narrative, "the news," that is given to us by the same people who oppress us and shorten our lifespan in the first place.

And, not only this planet! But they mean to travel to outer space to infect and conquer other planets and moons—misguided in their belief that they can actually do so.

Generation after generation has been afflicted with their same curses, they are brought up in it. Peoples' beliefs are so ingrained, they are so brain-washed into whatever category their bloodline already represents and the way to direct those lines.

The challenge in overcoming any generational curse is in those that dispel the directed-energy tethers which bind these groups of physical monads to their captors. Those born in into certain bloodlines, as well as those born into lesser trauma and more open and accepting circumstances—yet both human—are limited in finite linear terrestrial thinking.

And, you as a being upon Her have a duty—an obligation—to ensure that the parasites do not consume their host! Right now, between the fracking, the mining, poisoning the ground and the d.u.m.b.s-a hollowing out of Her, is so detrimental, that it is killing Her.

And, it seems as though the powers that be, in their greed and hoarding in attempts to control Nature Herself, want it this way. After all, they cannot wait to go and infect other worlds, other planets—to spread their disease and maleficence to take over and squander the resources of those places far away as if it is their birthright!

With Truth comes healing and we can not collectively heal on a dharmic level until Truth starts to become the norm.

Chapter 6: *Flying Around Inner Space: Fracking the Soul from the Upper Atmosphere

In this Ageless Timelessness
we meet again and the memory picks up
where it left off
and in the swift knowledge of such
we are and have been before to begin once again.
Is Our Cause the Same?
For if we should cross paths
We preserve the divinity
Between us, the thread
That binds us to vast multi dimensions.
For what purpose are any of us
Except at our singularity
Protected by our event horizon
Where we reached for the stars
Out of our grasp, out of orb
As a final mortal plea
To live forever, Is the stone.
As long as at the end of memory
There stands every one
Until each raindrop
Makes the entire sea.
Beyond Sorghum, dense as Sangala
Divine Entire Of the Oneness That Is

Ley lines and geomantic domes lay the pattern that maps energy vortices and their magnetic paths. Almost as if the ley lines have in them spinal fluid or blood of the bigger being we all live upon...

Our Earth is a witness to catastrophe so great as to rip the fabric of space and spin you like a top through the various possibilities of infinite potentiality throughout all of your timelines.

The evidence is there of the first round of wars between the gods and the Giants, the demiurges and Titans, elementals and the sentients—however one wishes to refer to the characters just outside of Creation that first manifested form in 3D. Born blind to light and the frequencies therein, Titans enacted what it meant to be powerful but with no wisdom or clarity. Cognition with no recognition. Sentience with no self-awareness. Instinct with zero memory. Impulse with no purpose. Purely reactionary.

Titans were known as and the first sets of offspring from the Earth-Sky union; and others, the offspring of thoughts from Her brow. Sophia speaks of "creating without clarity" and in the post haste of the swirling, rapidly rising waters, thoughts got pulled, stretched, and twisted.

And, in the aftermath, the distortion created by fear and instant regret magnetized many in Her wake, caught in Her hypnotic serpentine wind shear. This is something She is reoccurring over and over until the memory becomes fully intact. Through careful yet unconscious repetition, She will restore the thought until no wonder of other flashes in Her periphery.

All of this is a test of Her *attention* and of Her *decisiveness*—not to mention being an exercise of *discernment*.

We all certainly saw or at least have the memory seed deep within us of what happened to gather those who saddle Her sides. Swept up in the wake of Her confabulations—whether from a heightened awareness or diminished sense of the self-will to become any more than a planetary system. Whatever the reason, whatever the purpose for that remains unknown to even the most learned or the most entrusted with this kind of arcane information.

The stars themselves gasp and wince, flutter in the skies, reveal the dark spots that pass before them—hindering your full view of them. They dance, flicker, throw all their colors out before you begging your rapt attention to their existence: to make them real.

Stars show themselves to be more than pinholes pushed through areas of black where the light shines through from beyond the blackness. And beyond that, beyond the parameters of this universe—what lies beside this universe is beyond the measure of length, width, and depth and indeed beyond the measure of light itself.

Why did they live? You might ask. Why does the human race live right now? To what end is living in an inescapably entropic universe with seemingly no rhyme or reason, no point nor purpose, when it all becomes dust anyway? What is your legacy? For not one is remembered in the grand scheme of it all.

Out there in the oceans of the universe is truly an egoless, nameless principle and the mechanism to it.

We don't give a foot or an arm any more power than it has to be a foot or an arm—extremities have functions that do not require conscious thought, the Universe functions very much the same way. It Be and It Becomes, with no decisive thought to the process. It just Does. That is what we call God. But God is also more than that, obviously.

The Earth has done well to hide Her cataclysmic herstory and She camouflages many scenes by sand, water, forests, mountains, erosion—not to mention towns, cities, and highways that are distracting to the eye. You can tell what many things were by the waterways cut into the terrain.

The clouds emulate the forms they are covering when you look down upon them from above. The ice, too, takes on the form of that which it is covering—no matter how thick or thin the ice is. Flashed and burned giants are mostly covered by sand on the land and by water, which also covers thousands and thousands of ancient cities. Some of these cities are undoubtedly still actively inhabited. Many islands and continental shores can, to this day, be inhabited from the hollow underneath accessible only by water.

Many islands have hidden shelves up underneath the water up into dry areas never seen by the sun. Notably England, France, Japan Australia, North Eastern America, the Azores, Islands in the Tonga, the Galapagos, the Yucatan, Easter Island and the South Sandwich Islands, Antarctica, and especially Hawaii.

This planet has pleats that gather at the poles and bow out expanding at the equator. She's taken on many shapes and forms throughout Her entire. Monsters sent to Her, Giants tented Her.

There are different times in Earth's herstory but the cycle ends in the same way each time. An abrupt catastrophic event or events that caused mass trauma-death and destruction— Kali's Dance. Hemorrhaging the lands and the waters from the tides they made the Moon to align with.

And the Giants! Which time? Each turn of the tides people merely got smaller. There have been at least three separate occasions there has been cataclysm such where you can still see evidence of whatever befell a particular area. And, you'll find more fingers, hands, and toes than faces, skulls, or heads.

It's apparent also that the oceans boiled at some point in a few places.

One particular netherworld in open existence is now sprouting above the water, just at the very tips of its mountain tops. This is exactly where the Equator meets the Prime Meridian. In the Atlantic, that is why the four facets were brought together in this particular location.

It should be noted that only two of the original eleven apins/lpins still intact in this current space-timeline and have not been hacked or taken over.

Chapter 7: *Breaking the Glass Ceiling: Edge of the Milky Waters of Space

Time turns the tide and in who could She confide? Marduk that causes the commotion is poised for devotion, for unknown reasons, even to get to rule for untold seasons. Nullify the tender times under the heaven that allowed such treasons. But, then he took it, did he not? Hath he could speak it yet comprehend it, not? He sought an advantage to carry out his vehicle's driven plot.

Kill Her, drive her, possess her heritage. Hollow out her like a gourd, for it be a trinket on his chain. Hither and yon are the vestiges gone, Her next thought to chance, to clutch regions south and not in vain. He blew icy winds to make still and halt Her in Her place when he gave cry for the reason why he would ne'er bear a son.

He chose rule and adulation over autonomy and introspection, to blazon his cheeks with Orion stars, and to raise on his chest that which was never his to employ.

Tell us what transpired: why had he conspired to exalt himself Sire? One can know the words to speak of all day and night but, without wisdom, clarity, and humility one cannot translate the root gem and will fail in futility.

He wouldn't hear Her then but will he hear Her now? Without even a whisper, a gasp of stuttering breath, he brought to blows and, in Her throes, caught the icy winds and uttering—sent Her tumbling back like a top and sputtering. She grabbed the wind but found it entwined His thigh, so She held fast to Him when within Her grasp, She held firm until he no more and lapsed. Into the frozen affirm did he paralyze his form. She, still holding tight to his-ness—no son shall ever he sire to give the family...

Marduk lay claim to something that bears only his name, if it shall go on then who's to bequeath his fame? His ego was so inflated that his power asphyxiated every self-appointed foe. So, might is right? Is that the only way to go? He seeks to hollow Her out, to make Her a Vessel at His command, how hath he reign? By clockwork, by patriarch, by force, and seasonal extremes; never by Compassion, Mercy or Reigning Nature Supreme.

So, how do we turn this tide—overcome killing rulers?

Neither the religious, nor a warrior shall maintain in the new land neither caste nor class shall be considered—you're all here, you are all born exactly the same, you will all die the same.

It was when Maldek blew up, it sent Maldek's satellites and debris flung far and wide across this solar system, some spit towards Earth and contacted with your matter, weighed and heaved to receive the push that polarized our purple skies. This event broke the yolk and hermetic seal of the planet in Pangea, giving birth to your certain death, and began treadmill-racing Karma in repetition.

Mostly, you will see hands clasping each other, sometimes many hands in one place as if grabbing onto one another.

The look of surprise from many gaping eyes is truly sad and frightening. Happened slow enough to get several frames of a giant humanoid in motion, you can see before, during and aftermaths. From piqued to shock finally to horror too late—their final reactions turning them into basalt and slate.

Figure 81. (Google, 2009, February 3) Full length view on Giant of top of Heard and McDonald

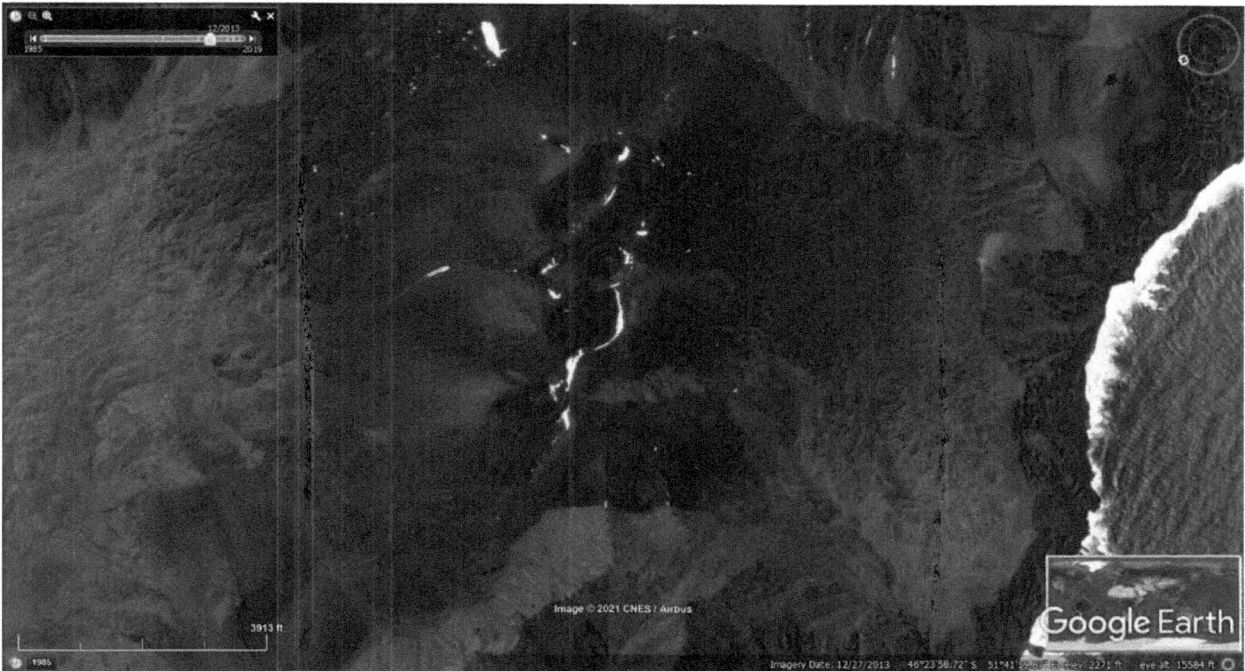

Figure 82. (Google, 2013, December 27) Teeth, eyes, the sockets above the eyeballs are visible.

Figure 83. (Google, 2020, July 27) Bottom part of head apparently cut through the face at the philtrum.

Figure 84. (Google, 2017, November 1) Could be a tongue or a thumb.

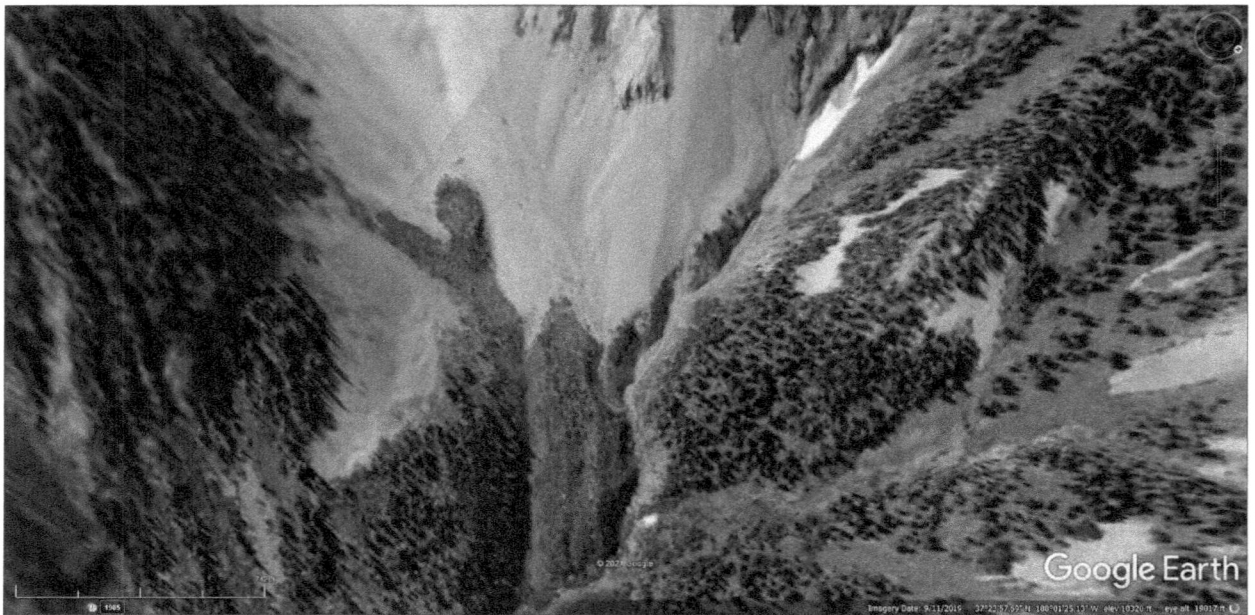

Figure 85. (Google, 2019, September 11) Someone climbing.

Figure 86. (Google, 2021) Teeth, hands and heads.

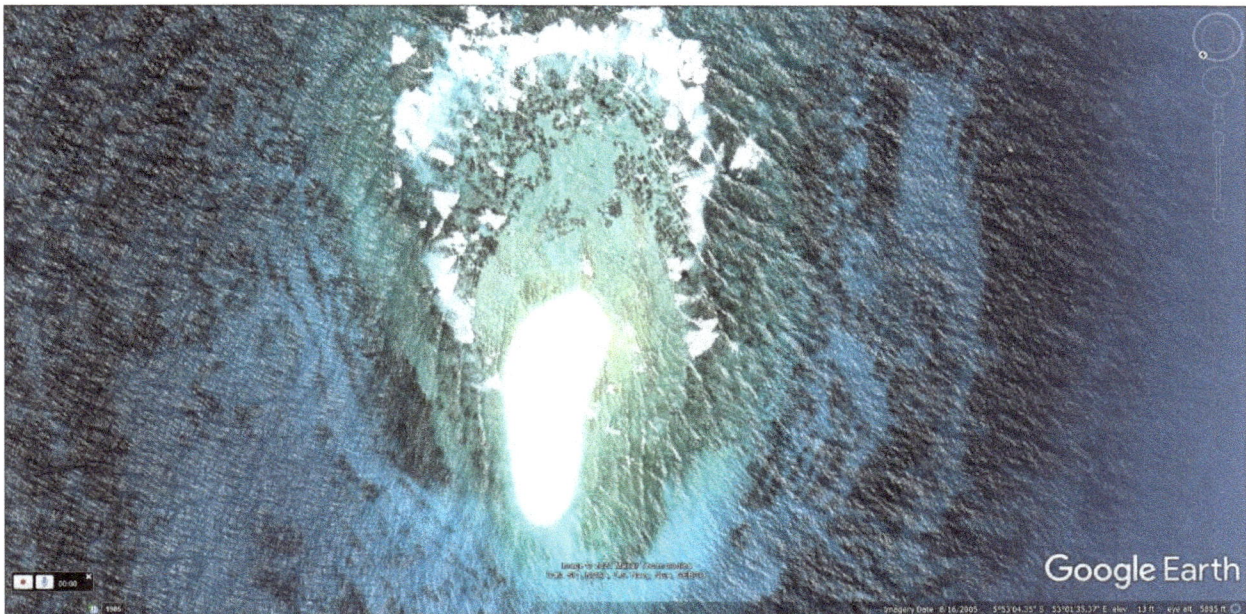

Figure 87. (Google, 2005, August 16) Underwater head with open mouth.

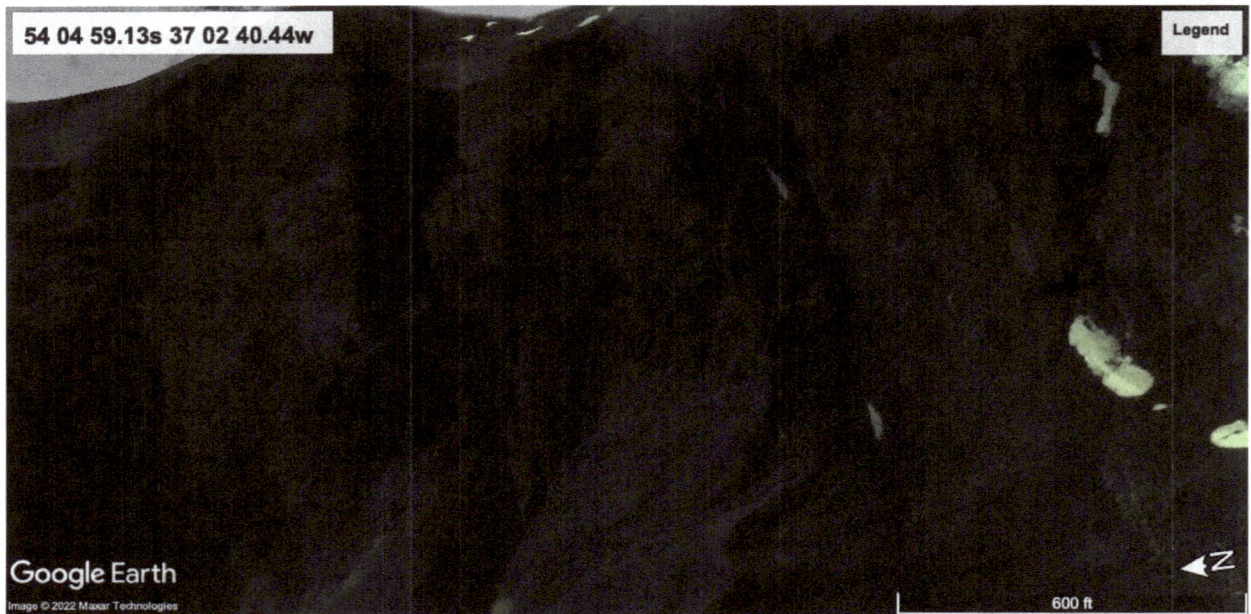

Figure 88. (Google, 2022) Heads on the cliffs.

Figure 89. (Google, 2013, August 3) Wild-eyed, screaming Giant with razor-like teeth. He's looking off to the left.

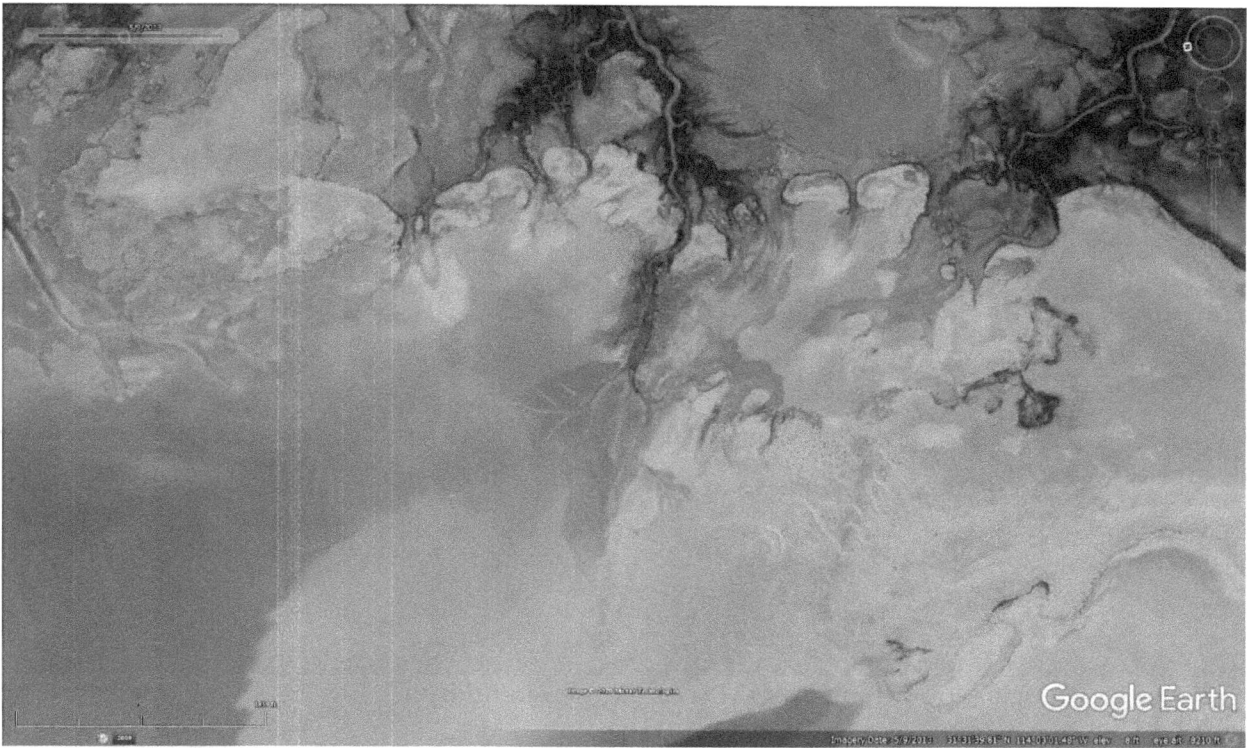

Figure 90. (Google, 2013, May 9) Fingers melting.

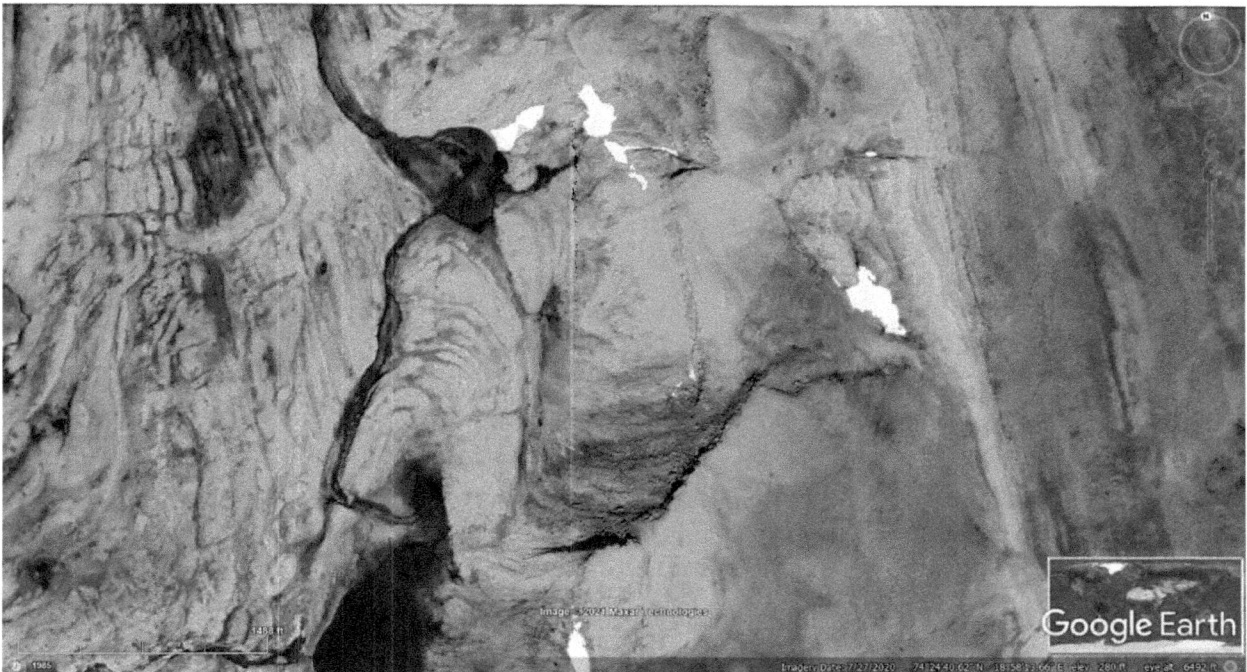

Figure 91. (Google, 2020, July 27) Two Giants fused into each other.

Figure 92. (Google, 2009, January 31) Looks like he's in midrun.

Figure 93. (Google, n.d.) Closeup of Giant holding the head of another Giant.

Figure 94. (Google, n.d.) Giant holding a severed head in his hand. Huge Giant's face in the forefront.

Figure 95. (Google, 2013, December 30) This is an open mouth of a deceased Giant—you can still see the uvula. Some small bodies of water are made this way.

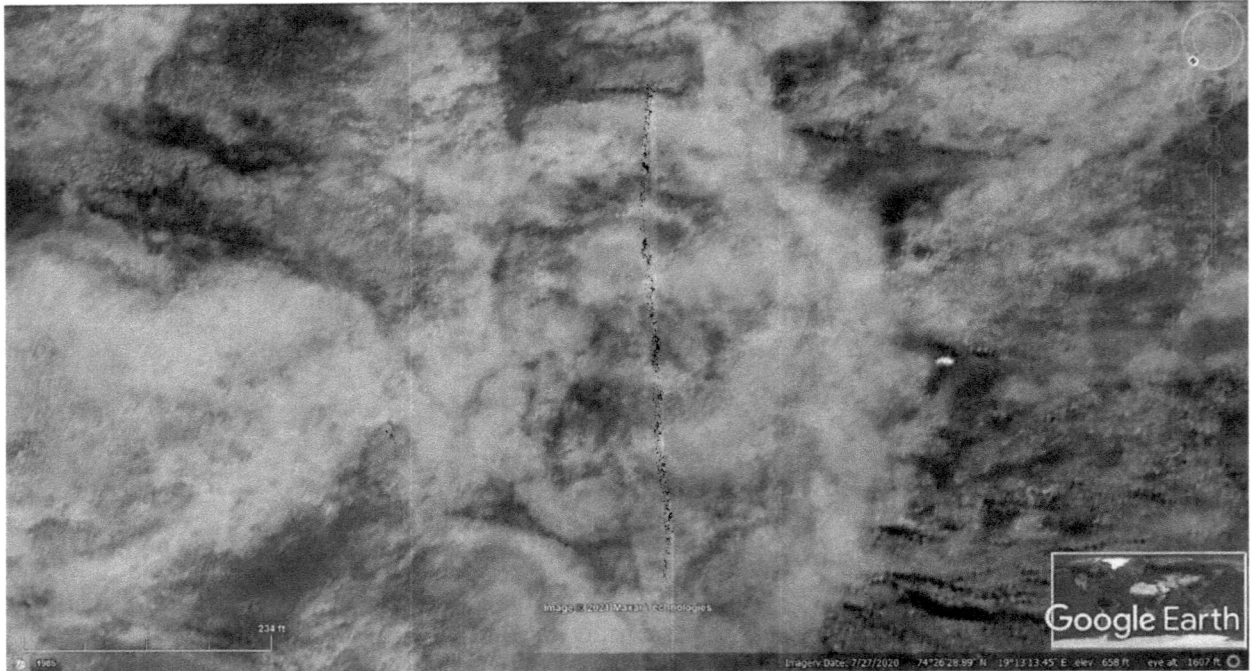

Figure 96. (Google, 2020, July 27) Terrified and twisted, face fallen off.

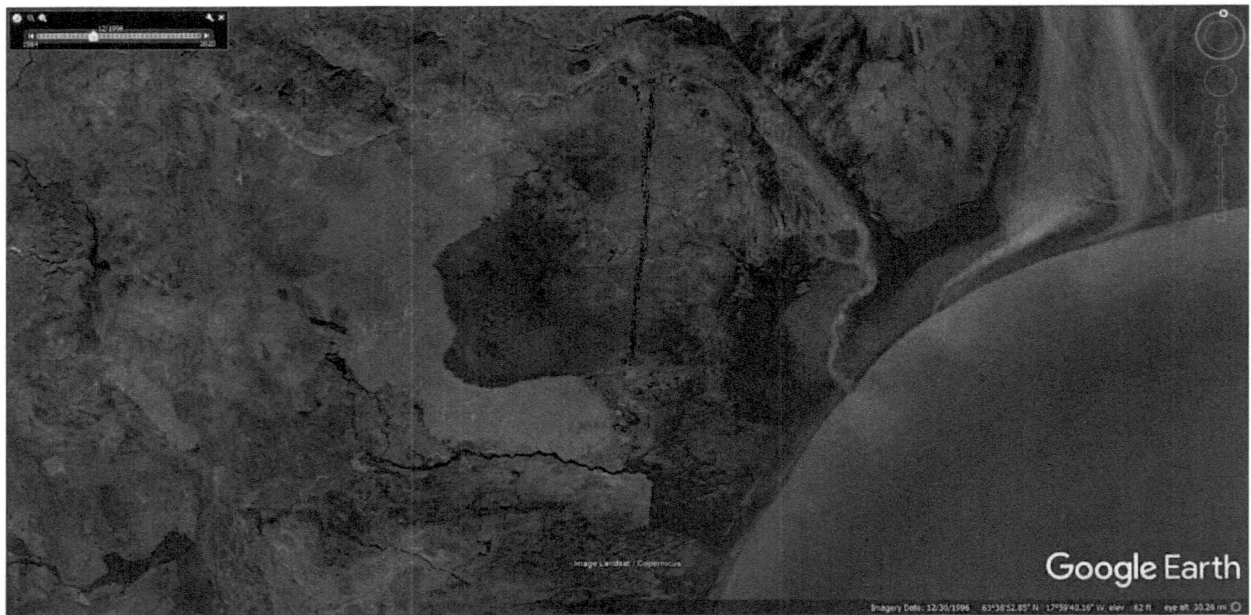

Figure 97. (Google, 1996, December 30) Profile of dark-skinned Giant.

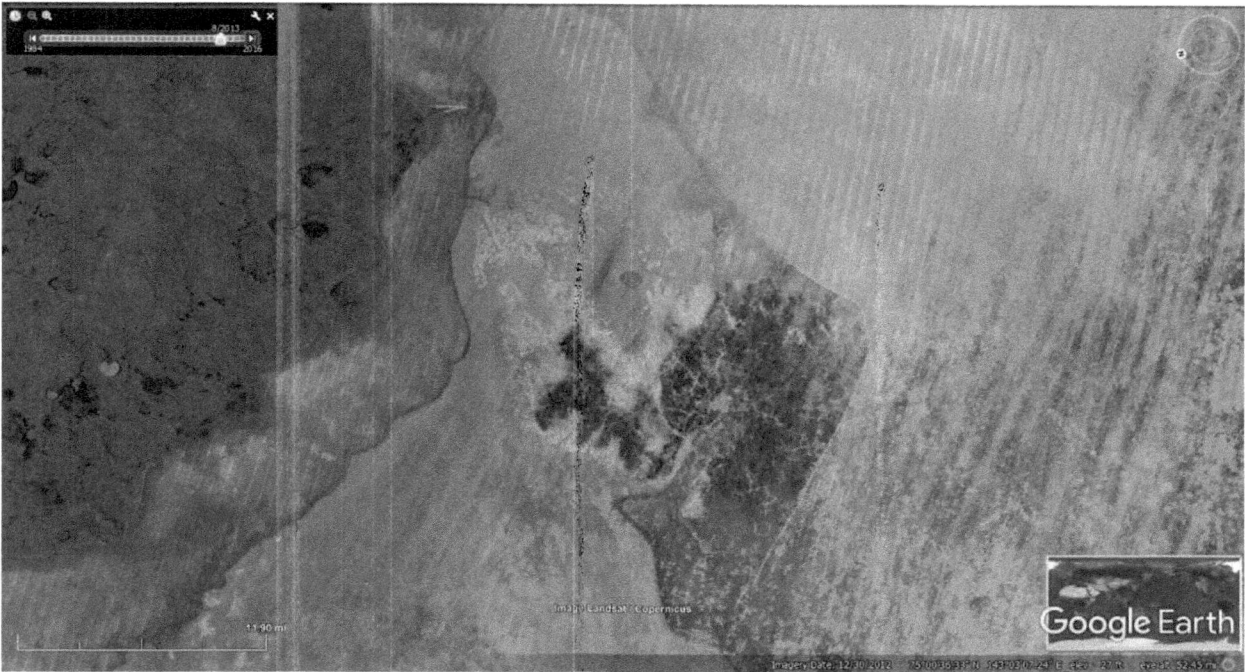

Figure 98. (Google, 2012, December 30) From the angle, it looks weird.

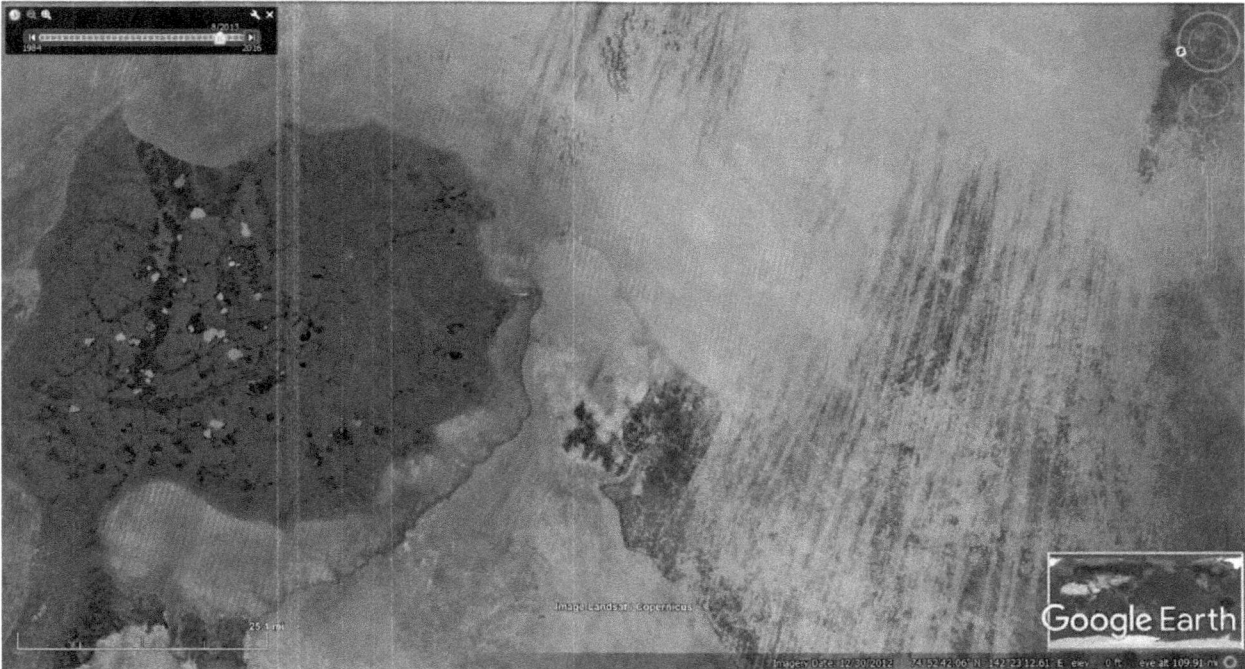

Figure 99. (Google, 2012, December 30) ...until you see the bigger picture and realize it's a Giant hand crushing down on these much smaller Giants.

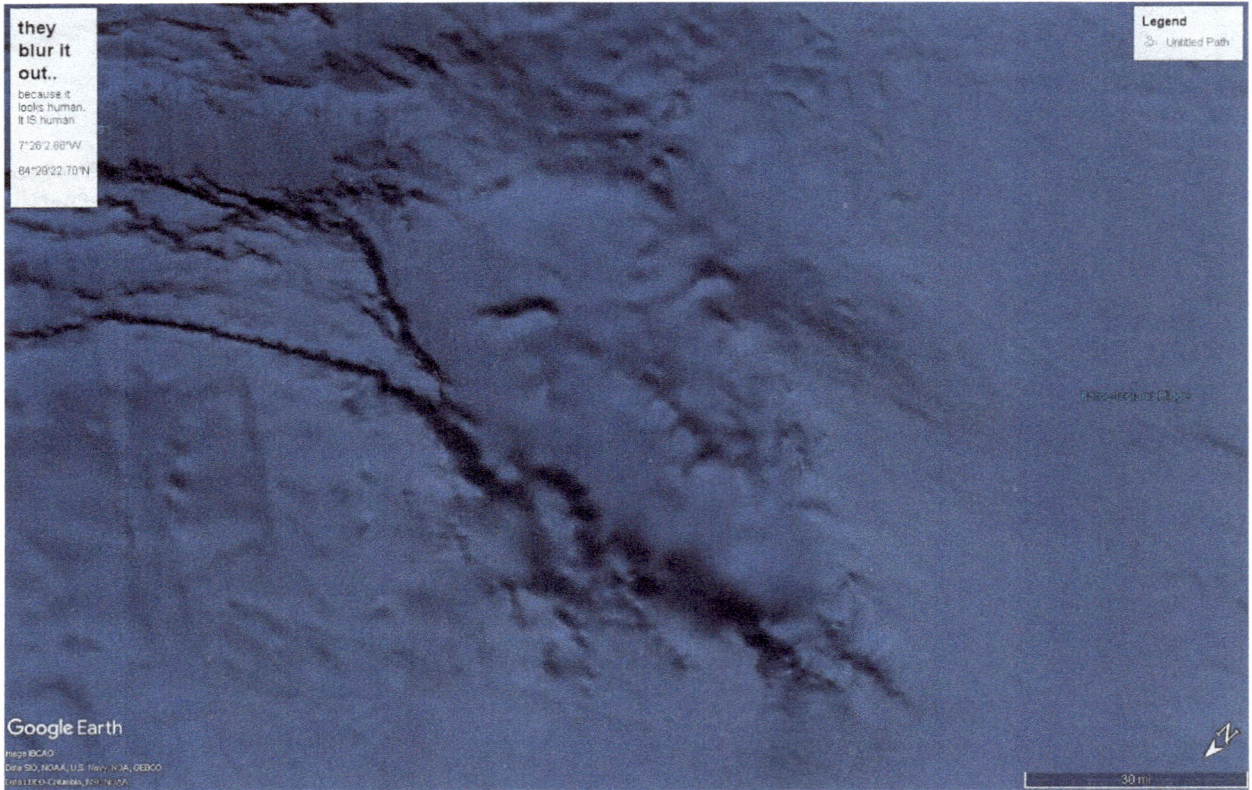

Figure 100. (Google, n.d.) A head that rolled for thousands of miles before it settled.

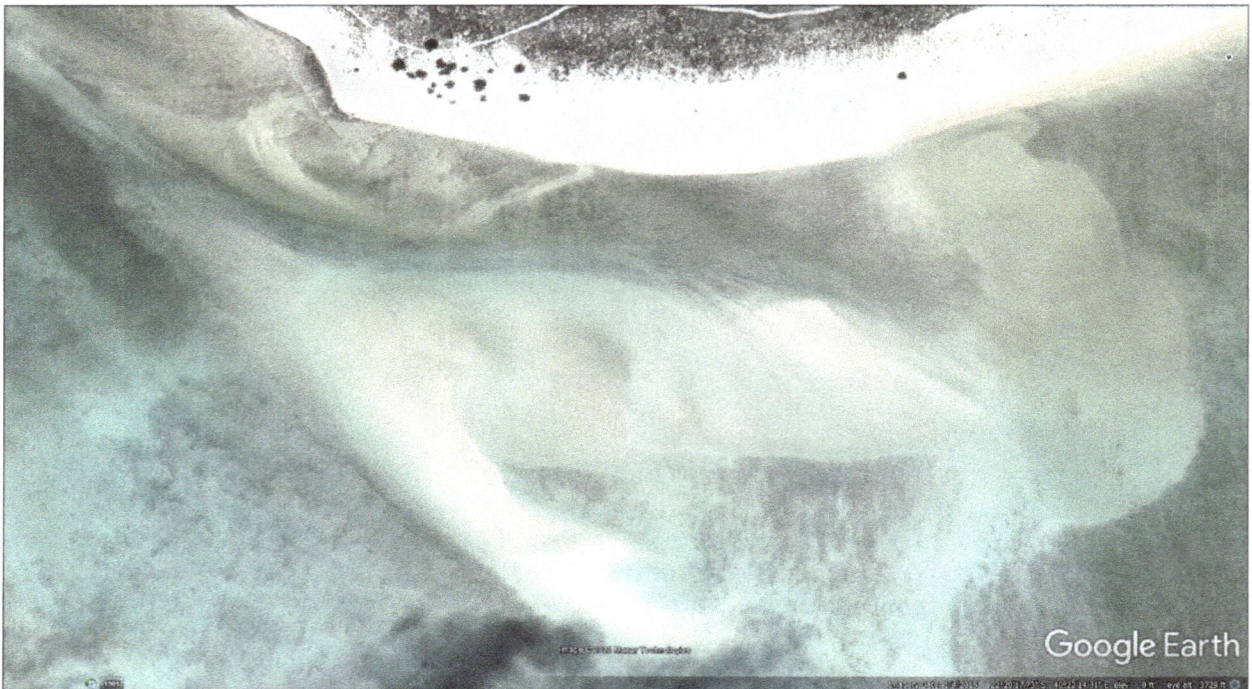

Figure 101. (Google, 2015, January 4) Two Giants fused together.

Figure 102. (Google, 2020, July 27) Open mouth and teeth.

Figure 103. (Google, 2016, December 30) At least three Giants are seen in the ice.

Even before then they (you) have lived, you have lived forever, it seems—you just don't know how to take your conscious memory with you each time you leave and then come back again. The trauma caused by the splitting that became this 3D duality and negative reinforcement in and of this flawed dimension threatens and saps the spirit/soul. It severs your internal link with yourself...so, you forget.

Each birth is veiled in low cognition—high imprint, yet little cognizance or immediate wherewithal as if you've merely awakened from nightly slumber, a dream. No, the scales don't fall from your eyes for 2-3 years and, even then, your first memories are likely ones built up around trauma. If not, then congratulations! You have been as correctly calibrated in this hostile environment as one can be.

Is this what is borne from tragedy? Is this why we are so traumatically inclined? Was this on Earth in our own past? Why do you dream beyond belief when there's no basis to it, as children? Wars, violence, death all fresh in your childhood memory from…not this life.

When does history cease being history and become myth and legend? Where do you leave off and begin again in full knowledge and recognition of such? Where is that continuous stream? And what will happen?

You will be presented with more things that look suspect but you'll explain it away—"Couldn't possibly be!," "There's no cover-up, you're paranoid!," "If that were the case, we would know about it!"

It is time—it is time for the Giants to be acknowledged by scientists. Whether they like it or not, acceptance of Giants' existence(s) is imminent and forthcoming.

From our vantage point, if someone is paying attention at all there are just too many clues on the landscapes and seascapes—albeit circumstantial clues but clues nonetheless. So many, it makes one wonder, or, it should.

The detail involved in many places where you can actually see what was happening at the moment of cataclysm is amazing. The Earth was scorched and people melted, burned, or simply vaporized. Each type of death is evidenced all over the planet; it's as if something blasted the earth so hard that in that flash, all is captured—like a camera taking a photograph and all that happens in that long, horrific moment is forever emblazoned upon the landscape and, more energetically, upon the ethers.

How can I explain this in a way that won't bottleneck your internal processors?

That will no doubt happen anyway! If you wrap your head around the scope of what all this means. Our lives are not perceptual crapshoots; you think your pasts, futures, and Presents (presence) into realities. And that truly is the Gift. It seems that humankind is unique in the way of being able to assemble subatomic particles into the manifestation of form merely from the thought itself.

◆◆◆

How do you think this planet formed Her land? Yes, much of it is the Earth, Herself. But, flanked at Her sides and residing inside of Her are others caught in the colorful updraft of distract. Whether witness to the lingering thought or merely caught up in the wind shear of Her confabulations, many Giants are tethered to Her side as if by centripetal force.

Chapter 8: *To Infinity and Beyond!: Not for All the Ziggurats in Antarctica

So, what does this all mean? You may say, across the board, about life in general, that nothing is what it looks like! In our day to day lives in motion, yes, this claim is true. Maybe in the case of planet-size giants! That is a ridiculous notion, even to people who think that 30 foot giants existed.

Well...yes, and they existed, too. There appears to be every size of living beings there can be.

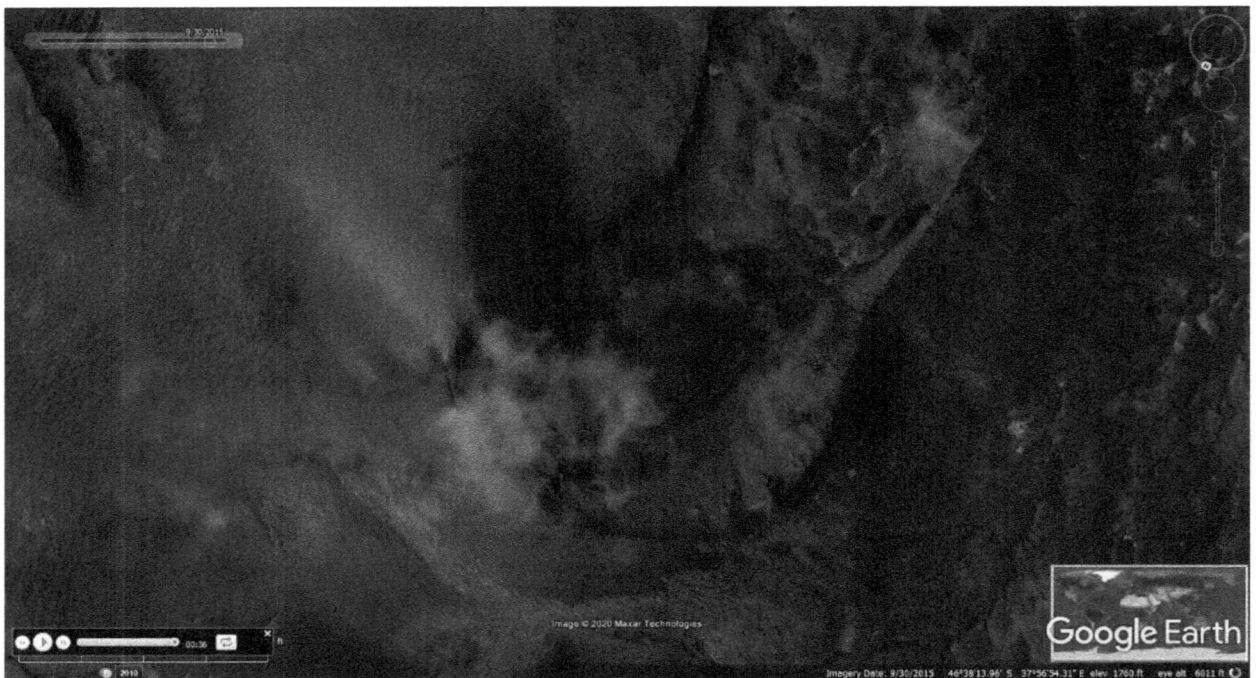

Figure 104. (Google, 2015, September 30) Hand reaching down to pull off a head of a Giant.

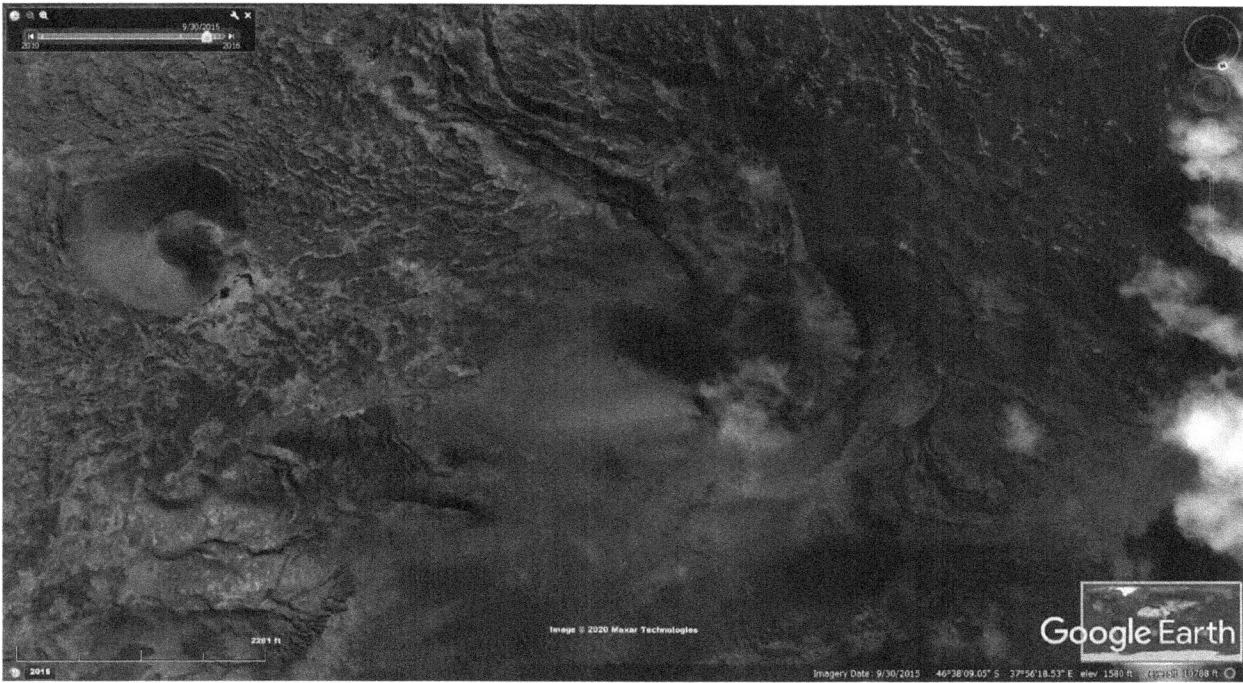

Figure 105. (Google, 2015, September 30) Head appears to be right where the body is, half the face (and a horn) can be seen.

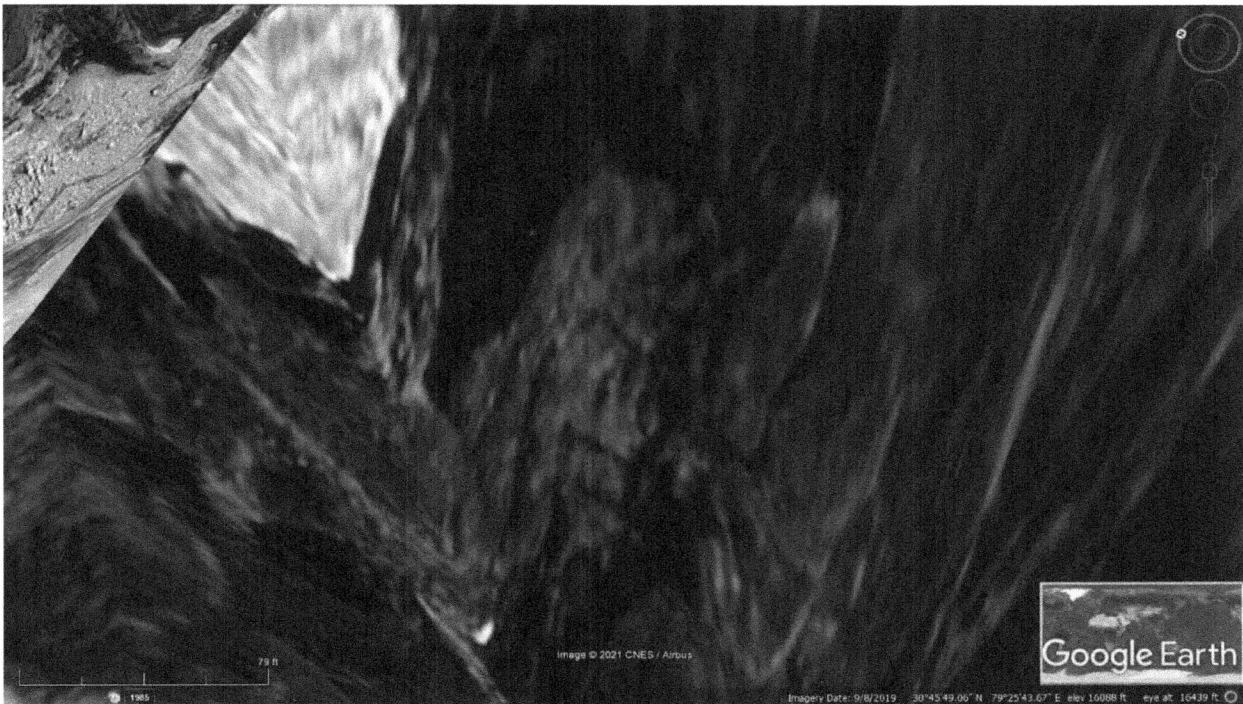

Figure 106. (Google, 2019, September 8) Giants hiding in crevices of mountains.

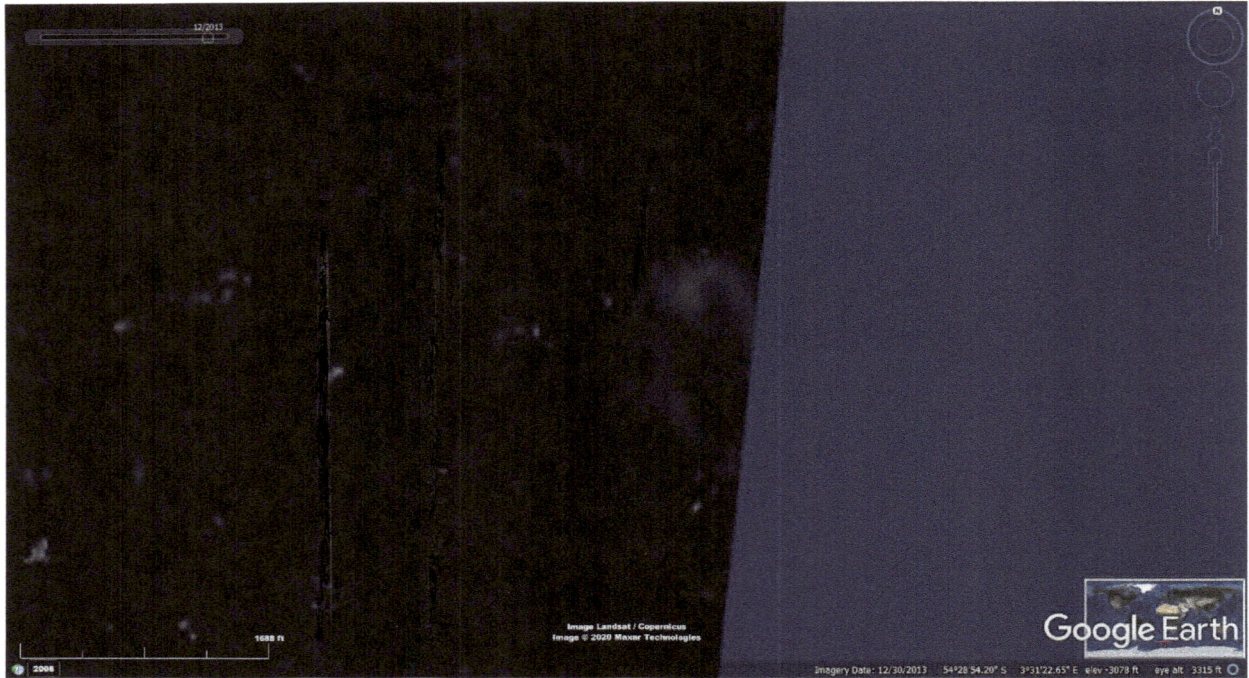

Figure 107. (Google, 2013, December 30) Not sure if this face is a cloud or a skull under the water.

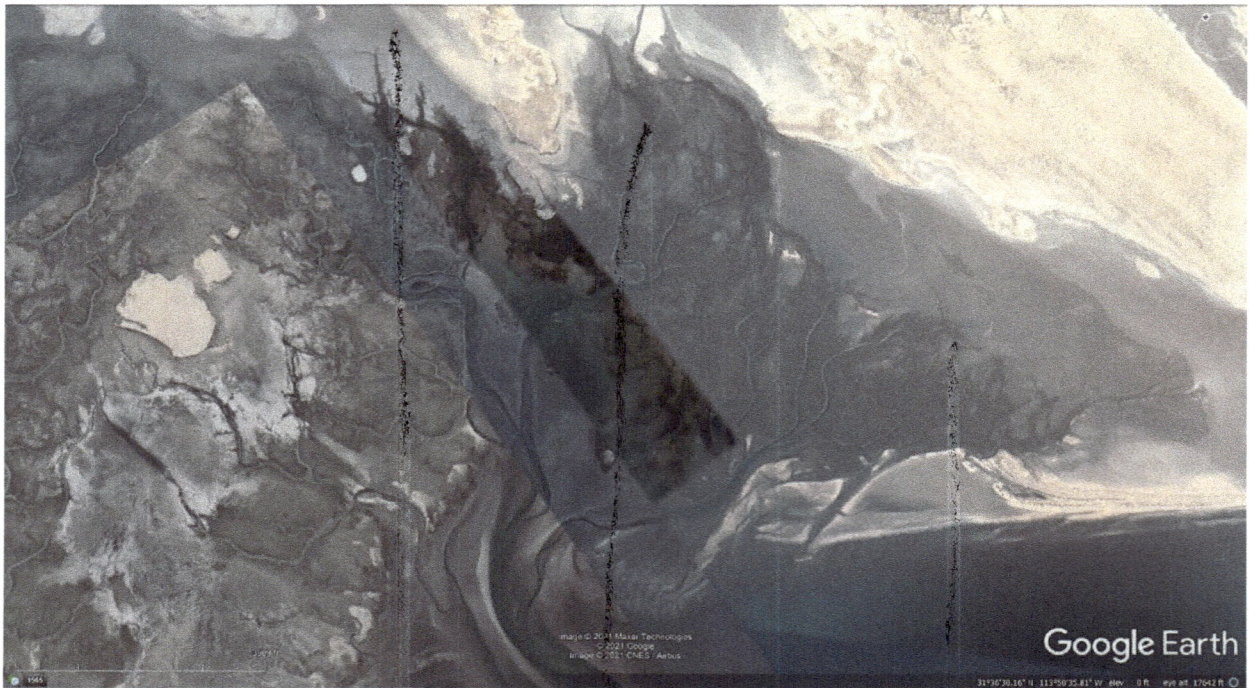

Figure 108 (Google, 2021). Looking back and running.

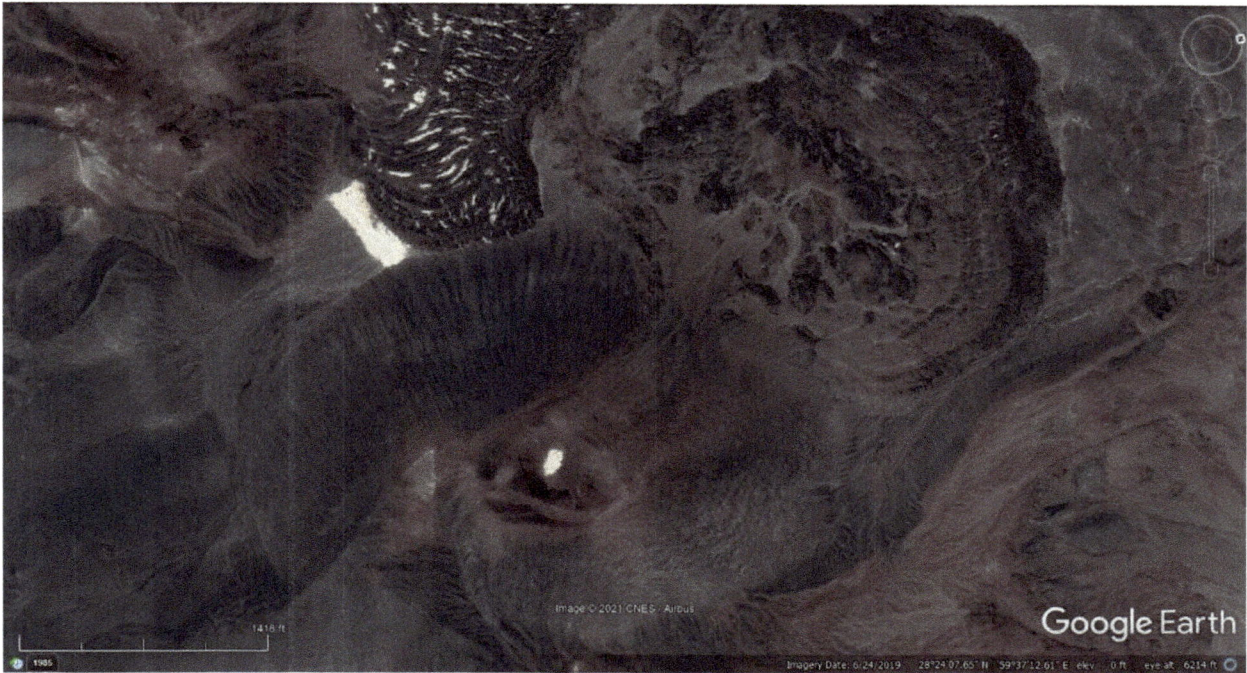

Figure 109. (Google, 2010, June 24) Coagulated blood coming out of this Giants sinuses.

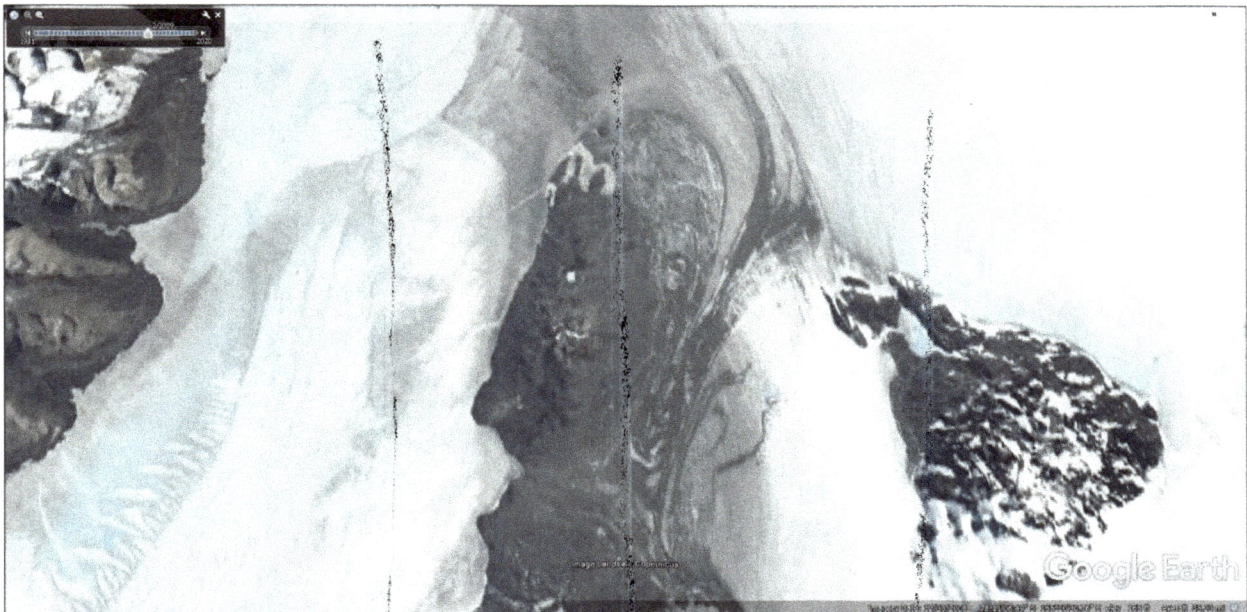

Figure 110 (Google, 2008, December 30). Two Giants, one getting his head torn off by hands coming up from the bottom left of the photo.

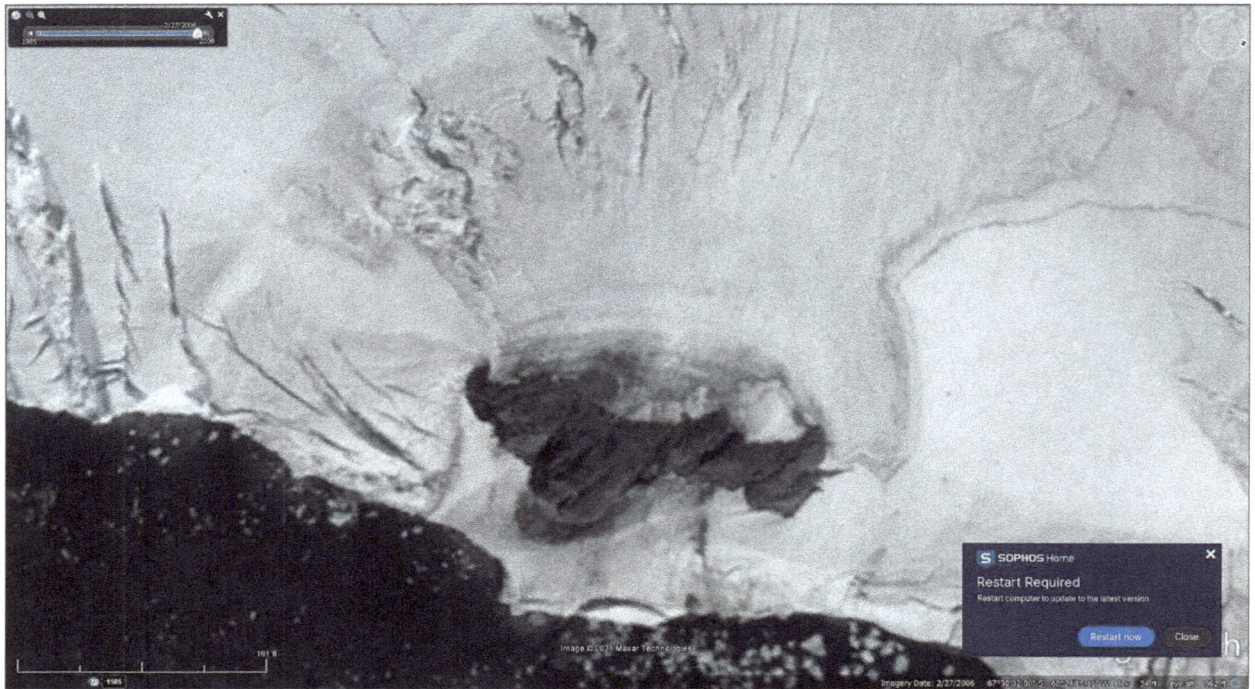

Figure 111. (Google, 2006, February 27) Cleaved at the jaw/hairline.

Figure 112. (Google, 2008, January 14) He's holding something.

Figure 113 (Google, 2014, October 7). How can this be missed? See eyes, teeth, and outline of the whole head, at the very least.

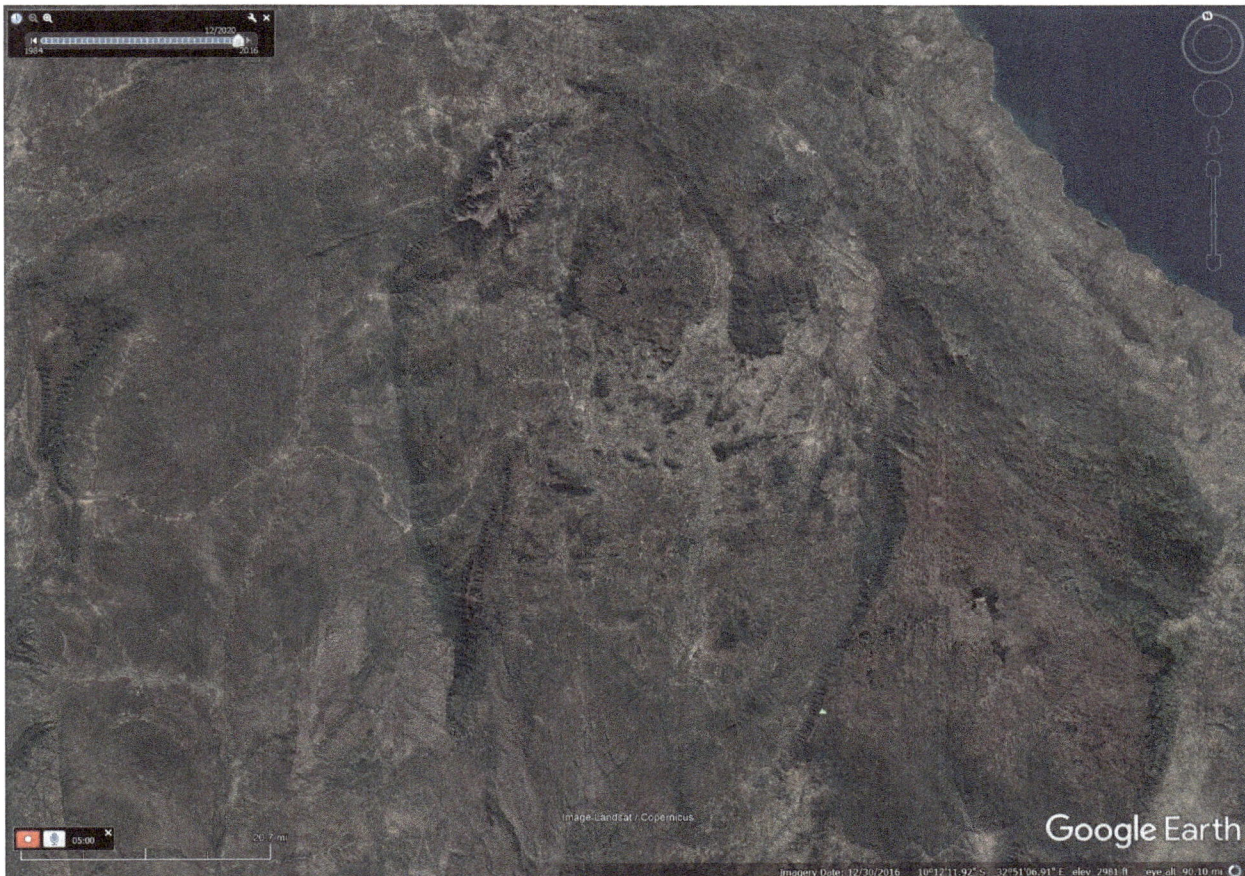

Figure 114. (Google, 2016, December 30) Dead Giant with arms above head.

Figure 115. (Google, 2018, December 14) Clear profile of tree-covered Giant. Giant's hair terraforms the landscape; you can even see the outline of an ear.

It is a ridiculous notion from humankind's myopic point of view where we don't even understand the scope and range of the dynamics and functions—let alone the vitality of life force of the being we all live on. Nor the scope and range of anything beyond the dome!

Certainly, not understanding that current human beings on planet Earth are hardly the baseline for the size of the average being inhabiting other Earth-like planets throughout space.

But, even presuming that the humanoid is consciously aware presents a challenge to the understanding of how they came to such conclusions such as making the supreme decision that they have the right to obfuscate any Truth.

How they came to collusively conspire to fool an entire planet of their same species of the bold lies and cover-ups in the pursuit of "progress" or—worse—in the pursuit of the meaning of life itself and beyond which is one of the things that, obviously, religion (and science) is built around.

I will point out that our reality lies in those that tell the stories. Except, a lot of stories I'm seeing go way off into destruction and not painlessly, either. Any perverse, twisted way one can invent a story and outcome has happened—in that there is nothing new under the sun. But what science "fiction"—if you will—or sacred text even out there is predictive of a healthy and bright future? None of them, it seems.

Is this another byproduct of our limited consciousness within an entropic sphere, where we have more or less collectively agreed upon what our reality is? It doesn't help when all those in authority are telling us from day one that the pursuit of money, property, power, and prestige is the end all to this existence. And, without a second glance to anything more. This view reinforces a falsehood about life in general: that people are not valuable and just what they can do is valuable and only for a time before someone younger and better comes along, in any capacity. It's worked, for the most part. Absolutely everything is monetized—this book costs you money. Everything has a price tag on it—everything has an evaluation. So do people—we are evaluated as early as grade school.

And, of course, the powers that be want to colonize other worlds—at the rate they are hollowing this one out, it will not be sustainable much longer, instead of people just stopping having so many kids. There's plenty of space for people; it's not as if there's a shortage of land. There's plenty of room to spread out. Big cities wreak havoc on one's dream cycles at the very least.

We simply were not built to live on top of one another—the psychic interference alone is maddening. Living on top of each other as you have zero space to do anything sustainable. Sustainability is going to be more and more difficult if people continue to get further and further away from nature. Everyone should acquire some property to live on but not be able to hoard huge pieces of land unless it is actively being put to good use for the overall community. Sure, a lot of property should just be left alone naturally. But, where there are people and families living, they should exercise their right to spread out and to grow their own food.

Everyone ought to move towards being able to do that—for obvious reasons. GMOs are no joke; neither are the chemtrails that leave a definite residue on the surface ground. The powers that be are attempting to control Nature and they are doing it! Anyone with half a brain can sense that Nature will ultimately reign in the end—even if She must destroy countless lives in the process. Lives of people are not in Nature's interest to save—no, we are I'm sure much like fleas to dogs on the Earth here and all Nature needs to decide is when to shake the little varmints off of Her.

◆◆◆

But, how ridiculous a notion is it really though when you consider—for example—the moon? Since its inclusion to Earth's orbit, people have gotten smaller, our bodies denser. Think about it, if there is life on other planets in other solar systems similar to the humanoid, who's to say their baseline for size is the same as our baseline? It wouldn't be the same, how could it? Why does mankind see everything only from his scale and range? How arrogant is that? Humans are so arrogant in the way we all view everything geocentrically. What we can see as large or as small is in direct proportion to how large or small we are in the first place.

These people who want out into space so badly—they have little conception of the scope of things on other worlds. Besides, your already lateral positioning in 3D makes it difficult for you to see them. Other beings who happen to share this frequency or bandwidth see you, for sure. But, they can move in and out of phase, as it were: move into and out of multidimensional realities at will.

You can, too, but 99% of people cannot do it at will—direct it or control it on a conscious level. And not many more people see these things transpire before their eyes and know what's happening. So, humankind stands relatively remote in this sector save for low frequency emitting automatons (grays) or those who are able to cloak in invisibility or those who can cloak in human form, using what again? Light!

It also has been noted that even with so called "angelic" encounters, those encounters do not take place in linear 3D. That's why one can "see" them but a person standing next to the seer cannot. That person having the "vision" is transported laterally into a sub dimensional plane; i.e., lower or higher astral planes of 4D conscious awareness.

A similar thing happens when daydreaming, having hypnagogic or hypnopompic hallucinations, and it also explains schizophrenic "snagging" of information from the very ethers of reality—that reality is objective "out there" but subjective "in here."

They say there is no objective reality but in fact, there is! There must be.

Nature itself is objective—it controls only the space it inhabits, it doesn't choose who inhabits the space and who inhabits the space brings on the subjective. Every existence is yet another life lived through the eyes of God or that which first created us. The experience is mutually *inc*lusive and cannot be anything other than that or else you are a non resonating closed circle incomplete shade without a "soul-matrix"—without spin.

With the New Age, a new cycle is beginning—it is time for many things to come to fruition. Time for truths to be told, secrets uncovered, and, for those who wish to go to the next level up, to make peace with oneself and others, live one's truths, and to forgive others is the way.

Chapter 9: *Dry Ice Covers the Netherworld: As Above, So Below & In Between, Too

So, as the New Age was heralded in at the end of year 2020 and the healing process of 2021-2022 continues, while it's important to remember where you are at and where it is you want to go, it's even more important not to be swayed into a path that others deem you have to take. What is it that you want to do with your life?

It's perfectly okay to not have a clue about what to do with your life that would bring fulfillment. At least you are open that way. Nothing like stuffing yourself into a box that doesn't fit and has never fit, heaven forbid get established in that kinked position only to realize 25 years down the road you compromised purpose and fulfillment for that uncomfortable slot that society and environment dictated you have.

You have to be true to you.

There are no enemies; there are no threats except for the ones who lord over our lives: the ones that enforce the letter of the law, imposed laws that have nothing to do with the spirit of the law wield false power that, even they know some of the laws are ridiculous, they are bound to obeying and enforcing them. It makes me shudder.

The enlightened autonomous individual will adhere to the spirit of the law. The enlightened autonomous individual is guided by spirit and conscience, is impartial, and is not emotionally charged. No favoritism, no nepotism—no "this side" or "that side." It's neutral, your objective conscience. A combination of mercy and justice. Most if not all poetic justice or justice by irony.

The unenlightened, led person will adhere strictly to the letter of the law whether the law is right, wrong, or indifferent. The "My country, right or wrong!" camp that says even if my country is doing something messed up, I stand behind its decision—this disposition is usually guided by high emotions, subjectivity, bias, excuses, rationalizations, and fueled by high drama and strong rigid conviction (any opposite, as long as it's an extreme).

It's all very, very simple—it's just not always easy. If you are ruled by your conscience, you know what's right and wrong. You have strong boundaries, yet your reflex is in the situation at hand. Some things are obviously black or white—either acceptable or abhorrent but I'm not talking about obvious immoral things that should never happen nor am I talking about beneficial things that have been unjustly persecuted by the law.

Your conscience should be the compass or GPS for what your vehicle (the ego) follows. And, if you approach a problem unbiased and impartial, the solution becomes easier—

unclouded by prejudice, unclouded by what their eyes are interpreting, unmoved by the movements provoked by and for an extreme emotional response.

It seems that the moral compass of the world is on a steady path south, but there is time (and a storyline) to save yourself from the claws of materialism and the myopic eye of intolerance, the uselessness of hatred, and the apathy and auto-pilot of complacency.

Robotically carrying out our assigned tasks in repetition day after day, year after year, decade after decade—until broken down and spent of our personal *elan vital*. On top of all that, we never know what our purpose really is in this world. So, the timeline and story line must change.

No more war, no thoughts of an impending Armageddon. It's clear to me that this has already happened on this planet once, at the very least.

Giants, they lay be torn and betwixt each other—stacked on each other by way of water, wind, sun-by virtue but a few lay where they did by design; their killers unceremoniously propping purposefully displaying the dead, carrying their own heads.

There are many Giants: warriors presumably with what looks like a certain scalp lock hairstyle and heads shaved save for a long lock growing from their crowns—resembling a cross between Mohawk, Pawnee and Sauk American Indians scalp lock and the Ukrainian or Eastern Slavic Cossack hairstyles.

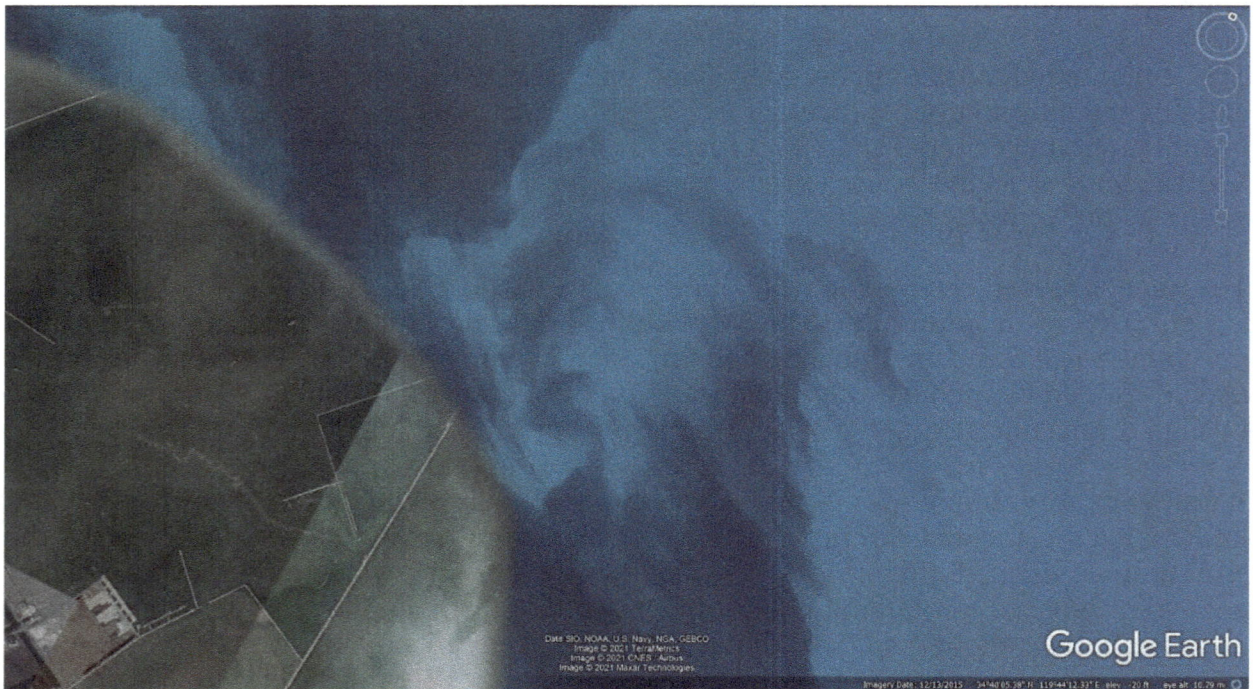

Figure 116. (Google, 2015, December 13) Cossack-style "scalp lock" hairstyle.

Many Giants appear to have crumpled down where they stood, became stuck in the mud, and died upright when the rains came or where they fell when beheaded. When Giants died upright, sometimes you can see how their bodies landed on the ground—at times just straight over, but many times sort of just falling onto themselves primarily in the same vicinity their heads came off and curling up in a swirl.

Perhaps this is the result of rushing waters as the bodies ebbed and flowed with the tides and when the waters receded, they left a swirled effect to the gargantuan carcasses. Some places look as though the waters pushed the bodies together in big giant slurries in the form of lakes, rivers, and small seas.

Giants attempted to hang onto the land but inevitably got carried out to sea, sometimes as headless bodies who got washed away from the shores and carried out just the same.

Many times, beheaded Giants' bodies appear to be lined up and slung over the sides of cliffs or, rather, the sides of other dead Giants, blood draining from their necks into the rising waters of the sea.

Figure 117. (Google, 2019, September 8) The headless slung over one another to drain the blood. There's a huge face on the left side.

Figure 118. (Google, 2022) More heads lined up and draining.

Figure 119. (Google, 2011, November 22) Giants slung over Giants, stacked up.

Figure 120. (Google, 2021) Feet toes and hands of Giants stacked and lined up.

Figure 121. (Google, 2016, March 1) More bodies, some with heads slung over the side to drain.

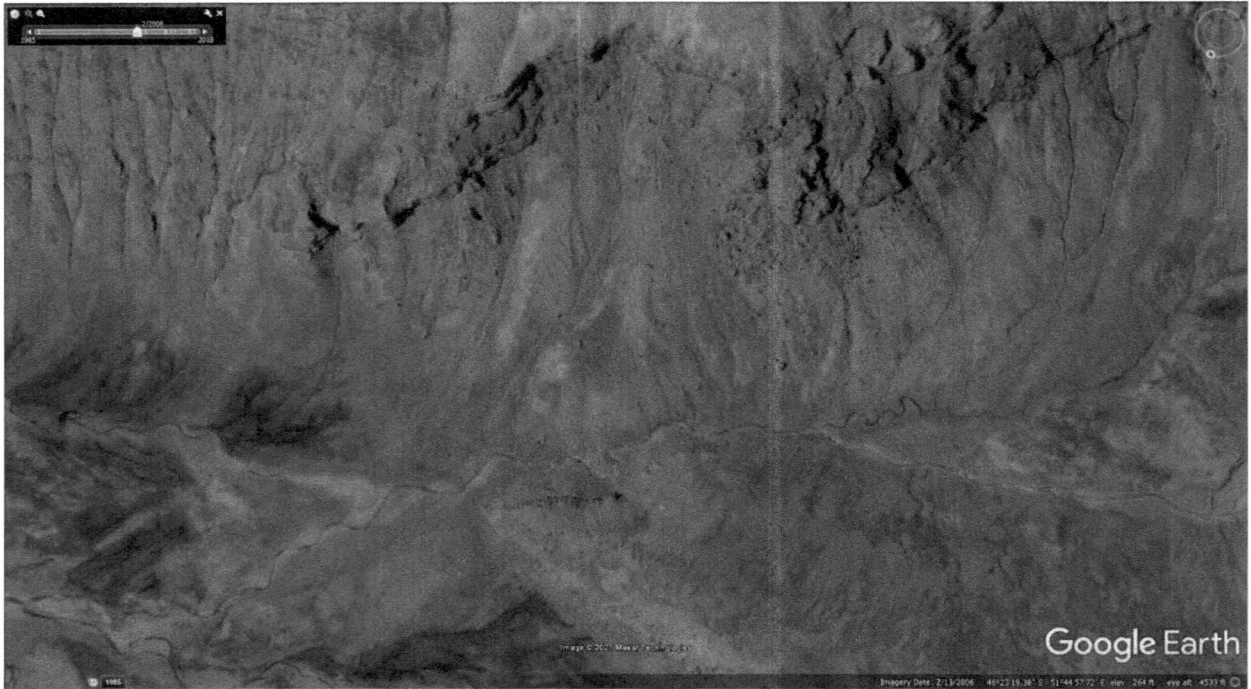

Figure 122. (Google, 2006, February 13) Legs, arms, feet and hands of bodies hanging and lined up.

And heads, so many heads! Some heads roll for hundreds if not thousands of miles—they leave a bloody trail across the seascape and landscape.

Some Giants are cleaved at just the top of the head, taking off the minimal amount of brain to be instantaneously fatal. Others are cut clean through the mouth so that the lower jaw is still attached to the body. Disembodied arms and hands or elaborate weapons appear from nowhere to pinch off heads of other Giants. Arms and hands and weapons coming from who-knows-where—because, oftentimes, it can't be traced back to the rest of the body. It is strange. Many scenes appear to be very gruesome, violent, and appeared to have happened quickly and were deadly—for everyone above ground level.

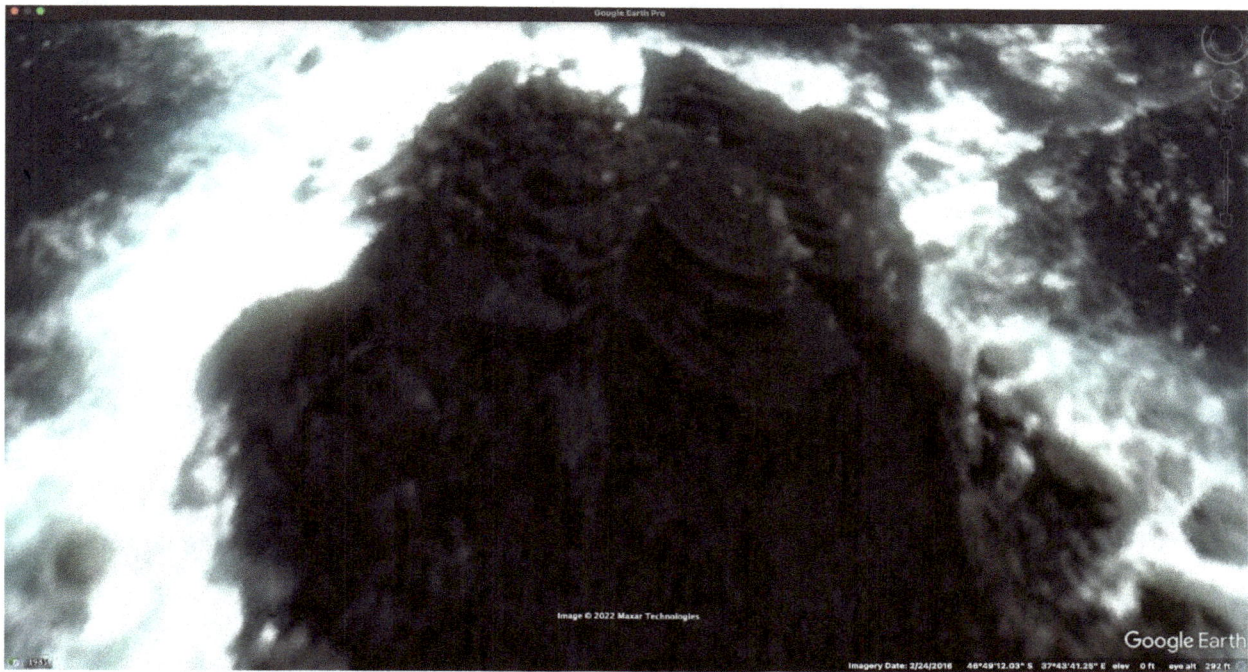

Figure 123. (Google, 2016, February 24) The detail on this Giant off of Marion Island is incredible.

Figure 124. (Google, 2008, September 5) Looks like he's holding a long weapon. In the foreground appear to be fingers.

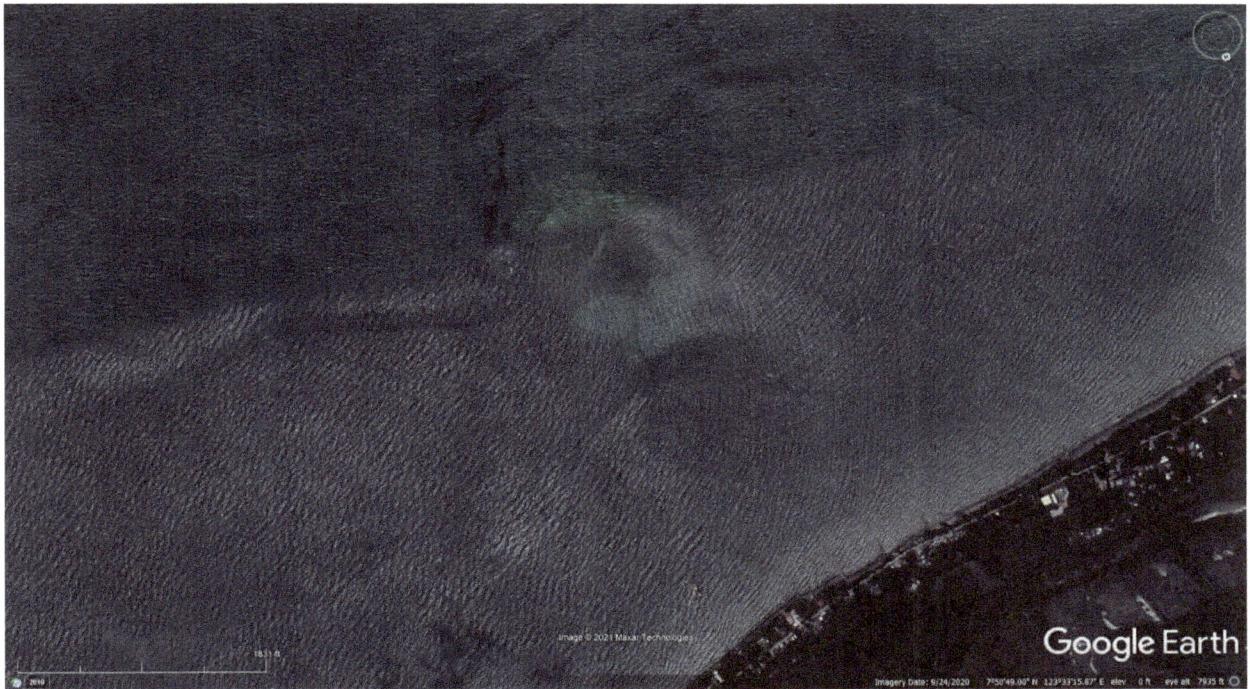

Figure 125. (Google, 2020, September 24) Strange face with one large eye?

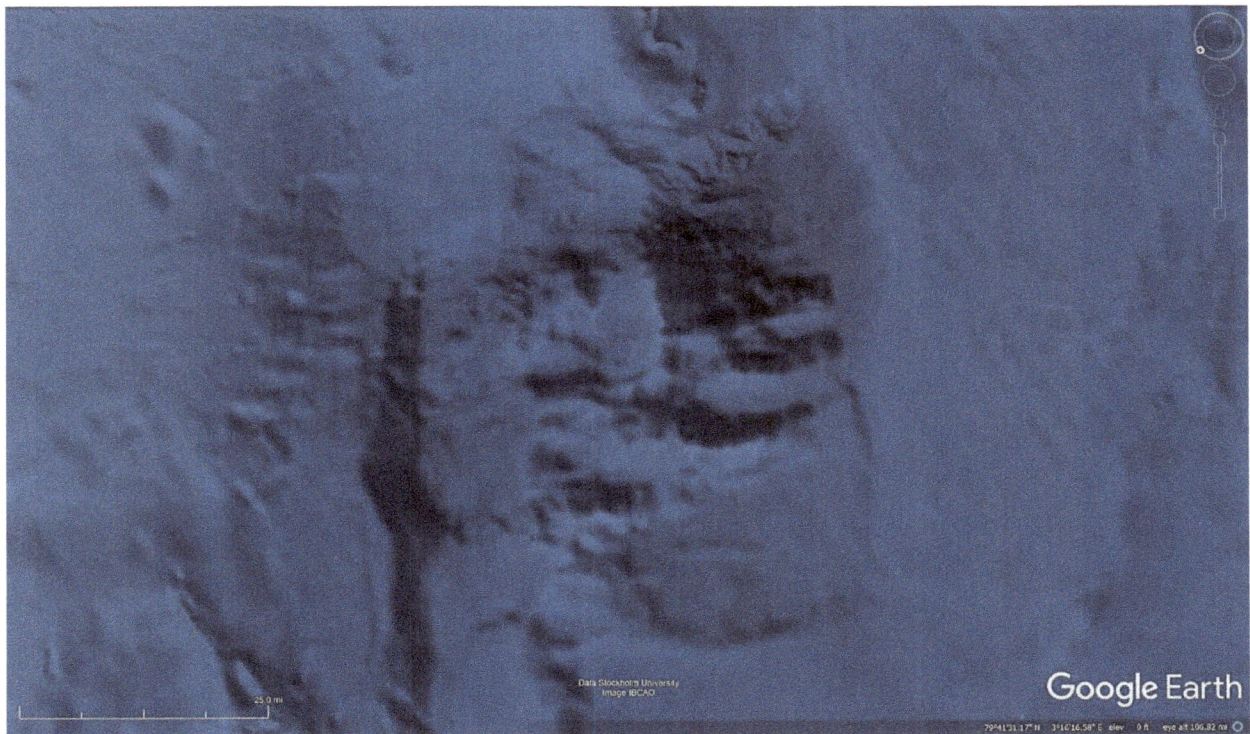

Figure 126. (Google, n.d.) Partial face close to the North Pole.

Figure 127. (Google, 2020, October 8) Bigger Giant next to smaller Giant.

Figure 128. (Google, 2016, December 30) Face down in the mud but holding a weapon in right hand.

Figure 129. (Google, 2011, August 9) Sea creatures outlining this Giant.

The weapon I see most often in the ice is a spear sort of thing: a projectile to cut heads off or slice right through and out the other side of Giants' bodies. Various types of weapons are present: swords, axes, scythes, and tridents (to name just a few).

In the clouds, there is the Vajra Dorje, a Buddhist thunderbolt thrower—yes, I know Vajra Dorje is supposed to symbolize a lightning bolt of information, sudden enlightenment, and such, but its roots—I have no doubt—lie in the real weapons of those eras that they were used in, say, holy wars that did have some sort of blasting capability.

Figure 130. (Google, 2011, December 30) Giant grabbing a head.

Figure 131. (Google, 2014, December 30) Looks like some kind of arrow.

Figure 132. (Google, 2000, December 30) Weapon? Tool?

Figure 133. (Google, 2019, March 29) Giant holding a rifle?

The Sharur, a Hindu weapon of war known as the smasher of thousands, is another weapon I have seen on Google Earth.

Whatever happened on the planet, it was far more devastating worldwide than one can fathom. What happened on this planet looks like a worldwide war and a slaughterhouse. Many seas in the world still run red with the blood of Giants.

The poles of the Earth, as I have said, preserve tissues very well and the ice at the poles is melting. I can only imagine what they must be finding under the melted ice in Antarctica. Ice is melting so fast, they'll never be able to successfully hide it all.

But Google Earth is not the same as it was. And, Google Earth being put on the browser where its visual capabilities are further stunted, will only further keeping everyone in the dark about the history of this planet.

Many Giants are in the hands of bigger Giants. There are 3-5 different various sizes of Giants, if not more. I'm going to go ahead and say that, obviously, if there were giants as big as what is portrayed in some of the Google Earth photos, their demise—if by a natural enough death like drowning where the body would decompose—would explain volcanoes.

I know how crazy that sounds but I'm not joking! You have to realize how big the first wave of Giants or Titans (as they were known), were. Even the second and third waves of Giants—and who knows how many countless more!—laid the foundations and firmaments of the Earth with their own flesh.

In consideration of the Nature that is before us, the Nature "they" are destroying, we shall take a step back. Either willingly, decisively, and consciously as a unified whole—spiritually uplifted, ascending in joy.

Or we can succumb to sterile, dead, and technological transhumanism—living soon here in biospheres as the surface ground will be toxic, where nothing will grow, the sun burns too hot (as we've killed the atmosphere too along with the trees, before the earth revolts and like every time before), and civilization ends in cataclysm and mass trauma, descending once again into a cycle of embodying 3D flesh and experiencing cause and effect of karma and reincarnation.

We are at yet another crossroads in regards to how we are handling our "temples"—of our bodies, of our homes and of the Earth. But I don't want to be hypocritical or in denial here! I'm guilty of not taking care of my own body the way I ought to.

Collectively, the worry shouldn't be apocalypse, the end of the world—Armageddon. From what I can see, it's already happened—a couple of times, at least. It seems that we all are hard-wired for destruction—maybe it's a byproduct of an entropic, finite existence or merely the realization of such. It also seems like we are incapable of rising above ourselves—rising above things like racism, classism, all the -isms that keep us separated from one another.

Spitting on those in lesser circumstances (by not sharing the incredible wealth that this capitalist society allows one to accumulate to hoarding proportions) is anti-social and even criminal—not to mention just basically disgustingly greedy. America is the biggest offender of judgment by what the next guy has and it's this sort of attitude that relishes exclusivity and usually some severe form of hatred; i.e., racism, misogyny, and xenophobia exists.

That people are truly impressed by what another has rather than the character of the individual is sociopathic and harmful. It's not so much that humans are negatively reinforced—although that does play a part; it's that people put more value on things rather than people (and shiny stuff impresses shallow people). Shallow, vapid money-grubbing billionaires know that without money no one will pay them mind and it takes a lot more character to routinely do the right thing; it's more difficult to do what's right, positive, and a leap of faith all without expectation of money.

Virtually nothing is free any longer and what is free is bollocks. One almost gets punished by using something free or you get the bottom of the barrel: the dangling carrot (so later they can gouge you for money when you've found that you can't do without the thing). It's really gotten bad only to get worse until oblivion, WWIII, or natural or unnatural cataclysm.

The most humane thing that could happen (as far as world wide disaster) would be a strong EMP to obliterate the technological genie that they've cut loose from its bottle in creating their AIs and quantum computers.

Chapter 10: *Shangri-la in Shambala: Turning the Earth from the Inside Out

Squares - Head
Ovals - Foot, Agape Mouth
Triangle/Pyramid - Heart, Brain (3rd Eye)
Circles - Eyes/Eye Sockets of Skull, Neckholes where the head has been cut off
Spirals - Sweat Glands, hair follicles

New knowledge of old systems for humankind to work through and assimilate in our own favor as the rings of Saturn begin to disintegrate, in this New Age that has at long last, finally dawned—bridging the gap between things that don't seemingly go together and finding the point at which they do.

Are we sure there are still just six degrees of separation between people since the popularity of the internet? Chances are likely that, if you are active on social media, you have friends or followers or you follow someone who—before the popularity of the Internet—you would have never heard of or knew about.

The Internet has enabled everyone who participates a chance to reach out to anyone else who participates in it and that, in itself, is an incredible power. We should not take this power lightly or frivolously. In a way, the Internet has given us an opportunity—maybe our last chance—to be human with another human. That is, before the eventual death of the Internet because of malware and upkeep costs or until they have figured out how to fully integrate and interface the human consciousness online or have figured out how to make the Internet strictly a consumer tool which seems to be what's happening now.

So yeah—before they let the machine completely take over, unless we are already living in a simulation (in which case they already have), the Internet is the one place where humans from all over the world can meet one another. We may as well utilize the Internet to do just that—if we have unity nowhere else in our lives and being well into future shock we can still take refuge in a place online; the Internet may be a way to bring everyone together even though they invented it in part to ensnare everyone.

If you are a human being with a conscience and empathy for others, you would not like to see people in pain or struggling—it would not even occur to you not to help when you could. It's just that a lot of people have been struggling and are out of options (and end up homeless or hopeless and/or get sick and die before they've done what they've come to the planet to do).

I understand that no experience is ever truly wasted but there's a lot of emptiness and/or strife in a lot of people's lives. We have been conditioned into this idea of scarcity—that's there's not enough of x and that is simply not true. When you have 1% of the population that owns 90-99% of the percentage of

- land
- money
- decision-making of laws
- the news outlets
- educational systems
- corporations that basically control our health systems

The concentration of money and resources go to black budgets, billionaires pockets, space programs, arms for whatever "enemy" they deem necessary to give excuse as to where the money goes—be they "enemy" foreign countries, "terrorists," "domestic terrorists," "extraterrestrial threats" to finally the governments' own citizens will be deemed "enemies of the state"

They will scapegoat anyone—we are all targeted individuals. The biggest laboratory on the planet is the planet of guinea pigs of every strata of class, every subculture of pop culture, every movement, fellowship, group-for-a-cause, cult, religion, fan base, team, panel, and every disenfranchised or otherwise disconnected individual.

One does not have to be an extremist to have a radically different viewpoint. And the definition of a radically different viewpoint (these days) is any that conflicts with the "official narrative," whatever the "official narrative" is that day.

"The system" is broken; it was set up to fail. It was set up so the few can benefit from the many. These are the same few who run and own the banks, run and own the media, run and own politicians and lawmakers.

Democracy is what they call it but, when the game is so rigged, it's basically a totalitarian state and its people are living in a feudal system.

In order for any sort of autonomy to happen, we must be peaceful and not in a state of desperation if chaos were to prevail in the breakdown of society—let's work towards keeping chaos from happening.

The severity of false flag events are getting closer and closer—the push forward onto the end of a police-state is obvious. If it is obvious to me and—believe me when I say I am trying *not* to pay attention—then it must be obvious to those that are paying attention. Then, I remember that those that are paying attention are being led the wrong way—the media has people so whipped up that they no longer are fighting for peace, they are fighting to create dissension between at least two different factions of people: any two factions.

Hatred, classism, and racism should be treated like the mental disorders that they are. There shouldn't be these feelings of separatism—but we've alienated ourselves from one another thanks to the technological beast that is before us.

The Internet is dead—how we once enjoyed it is no more. Twenty years ago, we didn't need to buy any of the stuff we have to buy now. And all hardware is going software—how much software are you buying these days that you didn't twenty years ago?

The Internet also with all of its bots and AI integration makes up about 40% of Internet traffic—so it's being manipulated in the worst way to keep us as consumers, nothing more.

Soon, the Internet will only be useful or helpful as long as there are paying customers for it. Twenty years ago, we needed none of this stuff that has anything to do with being "online." As long as we are consumers, the powers-that-be will continue to sell us products, binding us to a system that gets more expensive and more difficult to keep secure.

So much so that we must devote countless hours in maintaining some semblance of control but it's all for naught!

Stop electing people to office who have had privileged upbringings in private schools! Those people do not reflect the average guy; they can't relate. You get a pampered guy into office who has never starved, never struggled—how is he ever to understand what the average person goes through on a daily basis?

If you want a leader *for* the people, that person ought to be *of* the people. Not someone who believes they are above the people. Hierarchy is an outmoded system of placement and operation that has only ever served those that placed themselves high on such a concocted perch.

Why don't we hold politicians up to the same standards that are set for policemen, doctors, hell-anyone who's ever had to take a drug test to get or keep a job. Or for anyone who's ever had to do a psych evaluation or a Live Scan.

No, elected officials do not have to answer to any of those things and, yet, they should as they are making decisions that affect everyone on a fundamental—albeit mundane—level.

Chapter 11: *Escape from Moriaty: The Hollow Earth or The Cavities of Planet Sized Petrified Giants?

While there is a belief in the hollow earth theory, it makes more sense to see inner earth not as not hollow in its entirety but hollow in various smaller areas where a Giant died.

With some Giants being so vastly humongous, there would be many areas inside of a Giant where space is abundant. After the blood and soft organs decay, even more space becomes available—I'm certain that caves can be anything from blood veins to neural pathways to the insides of bones or intestines, any orifice on a humanoid being.

Many of the rivers that run throughout Earth today were started from the bodily fluids that ran from the decomposing Giants as well as receding flood waters. A lot of rivers bend and turn according to the way the Giant's body finally rested. We are told that the mountains get to be mountains when continental plates collide and slide up underneath another, pushing up the land and while that is true—many times a mountain is a mountain because that's precisely where a Giant or bunches of Giants died and the bodies shift and settle sometimes sliding up underneath a pile of dead stone Giants. Waters rush and weight shifts around letting things fall into as heavy, as far down beneath the sea rolling heads and headless bodies, stacked as hills and mountains.

Many times, Giants died ass-end up; other times, they fell over dead after their feet or a foot is stuck in the muck and they couldn't free themselves. Still other times, they were beheaded by other Giants and died crumpled up or, if a lot of water was involved, its receding would leave the bodies in a swirl pattern etched in as part of the landscape. It is apparent, too, that many, many Giants drowned—you can tell sometimes where giants were clasping onto other Giants trying to pull themselves or others back up on land.

Some Giants appear to have been eaten by bigger Giants or bigger already-dead Giants were made as hiding places for smaller Giants. Sometimes, you'll see Giants attempting to hide in a cave or somewhere out-of-sight or underground, but it seems as though anyone above ground exposed to the surface perished.

For the past two years, I've discovered more about Giants than in a lifetime of interest in the subject. But, really, it's as much about the Giants themselves but it's also about the other revelations surrounding them.

I am truly shocked that no one has compiled Google Earth images of Giants into a book, outside of Youtube videos and blogs and forums addressing this subject. But, like I said, sometimes Giants are so glaringly obvious that no one really wants to admit the most basic of circumstances that one can see for themselves to themselves—by themselves but in a room full of other people (where most get their validation for anything they believe in) they won't cop to their own gut feeling that that country or any mountain range or any landscape was actually part of a flesh and blood being—that's why it's not even an argument!

But, I also don't doubt that the truth about the knowledge of Giants is something we all subconsciously take for granted as truth, it's just such intrinsic truth on a cellular level that the argument seems silly. That's the sense I get about it anyway. Let's face it, people born and raised in the USA don't have those old folk tales told by the elders (remember, we put our elders in nursing homes to die alone often at the mercy of wolves in sheep's clothing disguised as caregivers) that impart old knowledge of things like giants. Our rootlessness is part of why Americans cannot unite: we live on stolen land, so karmically part of our heritage is withheld from us (and with it our ability to unite) until we get out of denial, get out of our right-itis and drop our irrational phobias surrounding other races and different cultures of people.

White is not a superior race—there is no superior race on this planet but, if there is, you can rest assured that superior race is not part of the human race in any of its colors. If there is a race of humans who are superior by virtue, its regents would not act as if they were superior—they would not lord over others, they would not react openly by way of "virtue," foisting upon others what he alone values as virtuous, wronging others in his vehement pursuit of deciding for others what others need and want.

A classic case of infantilization—on a mass scale! Hoodwinked for real, on purpose! Not that Indo-Europeans should be on our knees begging forgiveness for our screwed-up ancestors but atone for it by simply being a better, more open, and tolerant human being while giving everyone an equal opportunity for advancement.

And, to stop having this need to conquer and control everything in our sights—i.e., like our American government invading defenseless, innocent countries just so they establish their banking systems, ravish the country of their ancient artifacts and natural resources and foist the cabals governmental policies with our malignant, toxic faux democracy.

Democracy is a trumped up illusion of being open and diplomatic and power to the people but it is really masking totalitarian ends. Democratic propping is just as insular as republican posing. One side wants just as much control as the other side. These two sides were created to make people take one or the other! Get two factions fighting and no one's minding the store. And if you happen to not pick a side-by that, you're inviting both sides to gang up on you.

People fight when there's no reason to, other than to stir up trouble, to distract attention or to attract attention. Otherwise it's just drama and people do enjoy getting worked up over things no one person can change. Safe arguments are ones where no one can be proved right or wrong.

White is just a color—yes, you see, but white is the easiest to subjugate. Just like when you wear white clothes—they are the easiest target to drop some schmutz on, are they not? I don't like the analogy really but it works! Sounds completely ridiculous to my mind too but it's no coincidence.

Also, it is no coincidence that deserts are very light in color because of the color of the Giants that died there were white. One doesn't often see black sand—it's rare but when you do it's indicative of a darker-skinned Giant having died on that spot. Darker-skinned Giants are seen mostly where it is very fertile and green with forests—not always but most of the time.

◆◆◆

People's priorities are skewed when what a stranger thinks ranks over how things are affecting a "loved one." In these times, when it is more important for things to look a certain way than to consider the way things actually affect another human being is sick and sadistic.

We put our heads staunchly in the sand. as long as we don't have to feel it, it doesn't matter what we put another through as long as it looks good on the surface.

In other words, you could be having a serious problem but it doesn't get addressed at all until you become the squeaky wheel. Even then at that point, the quick fix is to shut you down rather than face it square-on and remedy the situation instead of making excuses why being messed up is okay if it's happening to *you*, as long as it doesn't upset another's cozy position.

Chapter 12: *The Future's So Bright...Behind that Dyson Sphere

There are strides being made in directions other than the hidden hands outlined in this book which show a hope in humanity—people building on ideas that will reform basic ideas about everything from

- housing with the building of earthships or tiny houses or yurts
- off-the-grid lifestyles far away from urban congestion
- sustainability that begins at each family core level
- people recognizing the necessity of growing from heirloom seeds
- reuse of "waste" material old tires, glass bottles, aluminum cans

◆◆◆

When one gets an understanding of where mineral deposits in the human corpse end up, the jump from there to the geology of the Earth shouldn't be a difficult one. Perhaps because it is so obvious that the subject and its arguments are circumvented-are just shut down as preposterous.

I mean, how long can you look at the "real" pictures of the planet and not see obvious signs of much bigger beings? The corpses of Giants make up the entire landscape. I believe there weren't even volcanoes on this planet until the death of the first round of Giants known as the Titans. The Titans were the offspring of Tia maat who bore them unto herself as an "elongated" thought just outside of the boundary of Creation.

Which apparently set off a chain reaction that has worked its way in like a crack in a bell that keeps getting wider and longer. Like we all operate within a split but that split also has a split—like we are getting more and more fractal, in our experience, in our memory, in life in general.

We drop down into our body—but how often are we really all there? Reverse the curse, I say, and take back your body, mind, and spirit—take back sovereignty as a flesh and blood human being and defend your right to be a free and open agent by wielding the power in your own life.

Personal power is not wielding over another—you give another person every opportunity to be an independent, self-governing individual in charge of their own lives, doing what it is that brings ultimate fulfillment while within the parameters of this society.

◆◆◆

But, back to the first round of Giants/Titans perishing, these children of the planet Herself, were far too big for beings of our stature to see. The foundations of the Earth which was, before that time, without shape, form, or density built out of Her and the many beings who were caught in the magnetic pull towards the Earth when She followed that Thought and when She was besieged by Marduk.

A moment of pondering—left the mind wandering and, in its own trap, nestled are the fears that you've wrestled with. Flesh is all that begins this—thus flesh is to all ends of the Earth in its formation.

We, as a species, have identified who we are—to ourselves. We've realized ourselves. It's about time we realize others. I am not so much only myself as I am another you—we've contemplated our navels long enough; we have just been connecting to the internal in the completely wrong way, if at all. There's a reason for all the cognitive dissonance we all have.

Our internal life, our "inside job" has been sabotaged by authority figures, educators, parents, the media, pop culture who keep telling us we are doing it all wrong.

◆◆◆

So, all that is matter is made from flesh! Planets, stars, moons—all hewn from the hardened flesh that crystallize and petrified under the black light sun, Saturn. When the realization and understanding of this monumental revelation happens at a critical mass, maybe that's what is necessary to roll up like a scroll this flawed dimension—spontaneous healing of the dark particles of light upon realization of the truth of how we came to be.

When one realizes the Truth, the options to know or to do anything other than what's truthful falls away as an instinctive knowing of the next logical step reveals itself in the surety and confidence in and of one's actions—a swift decisive and efficient remedy for one's hurdles: a flow that once you get into it, serendipitously synchronistic events give you the confirmation that you are on the correct (or best for the circumstance) path at that time.

So mankind wishes to ascend to the stars but cannot until we can distribute what is Ours, For All—For Every One.

And, not hoard his gold like one who's sold his soul and casts to the wind his humanity for riches and the land and calamity!

> 'For he is Gall and he wants it all, under his reign and domain He can know the language but interpret or apply it he cannot'

History will never be our story—your story or my story. And, in fact, they are trying to suppress our story and keep it a mystery.

I say we waste no time in this brand new Era of the Age of Aquarius—dispel the disillusions that predominated the previous Age of Pisces. Let's bring out into the open all the truths that have been hidden. To what end does withholding information of our past serve?

Control over others—manipulation—that's why we've had such militant upbringings! To force people into lives they can't even begin to have a clue about themselves, there's no time to wonder what, why, or how—just get these people busy doing anything, don't give them time to think about what it is that they want, what would bring fulfillment, what would mean something. Or what could truly change the world—for the better. Let alone how to affect that change.

So we've made do—going through the motions or not, never finding our voice, never serving a purposeful existence, never realizing the extent of our limitations-self-imposed or ones imposed by others. And, never realizing our full potential—not even knowing what it is we're good at—believing we have nothing of value to impart that doesn't involve money at some point.

Others may have convinced you that you are not capable, still others treat you as if you have no clue—none of whom have taken the time nor care to understand who you really are, instead taking the cues of their views from others who also, in turn, have not vested energy nor concern in your well-being-just criticism about what their own bias or judgment has unjustly precluded or what others tell them.

Even when there is something redeemable in one's actions to validate one's existence, people are quick to pigeonhole one another, to box them how they see fit so that it doesn't interfere with their own skewed view of things—to cast others aside as if there is no value to them just because they don't fit the mold you've conjured up for them.

There are those, too, who will take an attribute of a person and run it through to exaggerated ends—as if the exaggerated extreme was the original attribute of the person.

Still others will give false testimony as to either exalt themselves (virtue signaling) or appear as the "victim" in the eyes of another. People also often victimize the absent person—figuring the truth will never be known because, well, the other person is simply not there to defend themselves.

It's becoming quite apparent that the standard of measure of a decent person is one who is not interested in singling out others or pointing fingers or stirring the pot. Like I've said, the spiritually-minded person strictly adheres to the Spirit of the Law.

Those who strictly adhere to the Letter of the Law will inevitably become a hypocrite because, come on people, the laws clash with each other—they are subjective and appeal to no mercy or justice. These folks who strictly adhere to the Letter of the Law are the loudest and the most melodramatic in stating their cases. Good rule of thumb is: if you find yourself getting too emotional over issues—like feeling really strong *hate*—then there is a problem. And the problem is you.

But your anger is displaced because your oppressor has successfully convinced you of your role and how you are to play it. And, because getting angry at the oppressor is not politically correct or proper, having the courage to stand up for yourself may well upend you or get you cut off from the comforts to which you've grown accustomed. You'll bear the psychological damage after all, you've been told how much of a problem you are and you believe it. One tyrant for another. And ya wanna talk about others taking the path of least resistance...suffer a tyrant to secure your job, room and board and anyone who points this out is the contentious one? Pshaw.

An individual with honor respects others choices, wishes, and plans and does not coerce, guilt trip, shame, belittle or control others into looking a certain way. The narcissistic personality is a severe and rigid one and no one can live up to some impossible and deluded idea of perfection that can never be attained in this realm.
Within the issue is something you're either in denial about or cannot grapple maturely with—that you feel you must be the squeakiest wheel to loudly proclaim just how you are door-slamming anyone near or far who disagrees.

Not creating a dialogue, a mature and deliberate dialogue with those who would oppose, is robbing both sides of much needed empathy, compassion and perspective that—if not done on a consciously evolving level—works its way through the subconscious and out in most humbling if not humiliating ways. Your case may not be with the same situation and players as others but the points make themselves clear eventually.

I suggest a conscious shift towards autonomy: empty the cities back into small villages, be contrite before Nature—we collectively have cut ourselves off from it, which will no doubt prove to be detrimental to the "natural," free range, non-GMO human being.

The following paragraph is meant to be humorously absurd: people talk about "stupid tax" taxing people for doing stupid things—well, okay, but only if we can have a "smart tax"—start taxing geniuses! It's less subjective and, honestly, a sounder move; besides, they probably will be making the most money. But then, who's to say who's stupid or smart? Each and every one of us has the capacity for both and I point this out because it's all ridiculous, anyway: taxes, laws, the justice system, money, everything is external—our information, our validation, our values, our self-worth is all contingent upon just being counted as a member of the tribe. Seeking acceptance only to court rejection.

Remember when freedom meant exactly that? Precious freedom nowadays must be bought. Period. And it's outrageously expensive to buy and pay for one's freedom. Not just in money. Your blood, sweat, life force, stress, health, will, drive, intent all at varying levels

I, for one, despise money. (And, that, according to most people, would fall under stupid tax. Tax me!). It's not money's fault; money in-and-of-itself is not bad. I despise the fact that money is necessary for survival in the Western world and I really loathe the lengths people will go to to get it and justify whatever means in attaining it. A society that judges a person on how much they have is despicable. As if good character is inherent the more money one has!

People are so cued to judge visually, that's why they look only at the appearance of things, because anyone can alter their appearance for however long. It seems more difficult for the average person to be just who they are with no filters, in a crowd. People are always on their best behavior in a throng of people. But if mayhem were to happen, much of the time people will react violently if they are operating from an animal base.

Perhaps getting people desensitized to trauma, especially in crowds is a way to control them too. No wonder no one bats an eye to the growing problems in society such as homelessness, rampant mental dysfunction due in part I'm sure, to having to wear masks and have filters in place because it's the polite thing to do and it squelches our natural personalities and is in fact, disingenuous.

Why are social masks even necessary, at all? This goes back to restraint—the same restraint that enables autonomy. If one can't even exercise the restraint that autonomy requires, then one surely needs to have those masks firmly in place. It's all nicey-nice on the outside—where everyone can see but you don't really know what is really felt on the inside (because politeness and social masking has got everyone lying and withholding the truth in lieu of "not wanting to hurt someone's feelings" or avoiding making someone angry). But I'm here to tell you that, although the truth may hurt, a lie hurts a lot worse and for a lot longer—plus it comes with the disappointment of not being able to trust the word of another.

However, considering the sources of these external validations there's perhaps little love lost—after all, if no one sees eye to eye to begin with (because everyone competes even when it's not necessary). This makes real competition a power struggle instead, and I know this society values winning over peace—but what is there to win?

Your point? Independence but still on the grid—plugged into a life support machine? Financial gain to elevate only those who agree with you—or even give attention to at all? No one can agree to disagree and have it be cool. Everyone's going to be somebody else's tool because no one can think for themselves. People will distance themselves from others whose opinions differ from theirs as if—*as if* what they are arguing about matters anyway. Because no matter what, we all are being conditioned. We all have normalized a bunch of wrong things. We are *all* targeted individuals.

Such as the valuation of money: like what you have is who you are, like what you look like is who you are, like putting emphasis on external things—looking to trendy pop culture for meaning and substance.

If you are getting your information from mainstream media then you virtually know zero. Mainstream media is a dog-and-pony show. Period. As far into that narrative you've gone and it's just as intense and time consuming to deprogram yourself of all that propaganda and not let yourself be triggered by the veritable lies and manipulations of the news or as

Fox deems themselves: "News Entertainment". It's not like any of the media outlets are concealing what they are, they say it right to your face.

The mainstream media's job is to distract you from deeper issues and events that conveniently coincide with false flags. Their job is to stir the pot so that there is always someone to point fingers at (victim or perpetrator) and it's always 180 degrees from where the problems really are—they keep us all at odds with each other. Peace doesn't sell news.

Like: let's focus on some social epidemic such as mental illness and stigmatize the crisis around that instead of dismantling these pharmaceutical companies who make negligible—no, downright dangerous killer drugs that only exacerbate the original malady, "But wait!.." plus now with more side effects!

It is time to step back from the momentum of technological convenience. Convenience that is making decisions over everything, levying the kind of control that allows no *phi*, no fair divide, no painstaking salve—only obsession with compulsion, the record is stuck in a groove to repetition.

The most *humane* disaster on a mass scale would be an EMP. Sure, let them figure it all out again! The technological beast must be stopped. They obviously cannot be trusted—billionaires wanting to use the moon to dump our trash on. Just because the moon is essentially a hollowed out corpse doesn't make it a landfill!

You'd think these moguls would get a kick out of —I don't know—say, take a billion of those dollars and drop it from their rockets to starving people below—at least on their way out to space just to spin around the Earth a few times. Okay, the idea is ridiculous but so is what they do—to what end does it serve?

Why is it permissible for these guys to do whatever they want just because they have the money? The bottom line is that there is no cap on capitalism and it'll be the death of all of us yet. Capitalism, convenience, and arrogance.

No one person should have that kind of power—to be able to buy huge parcels of land just to hoard it. The extreme accumulation of anything is called hoarding and these guys are the worst at accumulation and waste; the more that is accumulated, the more that is wasted. These guys aren't vested in efficiency—that is saved for those they employ.

Why does it seem that people are hardwired for Armageddon? Expecting that "the End" is imminent, that humankind is forever at the 11th hour? The powers that be have the apocalypse—just like a life of prosperity as a dangling carrot out of reach but looming in the undercurrents of all we do.

Why does it take mass trauma to evolve, instead of by our own singular conscious decision?

When will we awaken to the lucid dream of life connecting to the consciousness that remembers all the parallels and paradigms, across all timelines? When will we give credence to that which is within us, including every answer to every question we've ever had?

How do we alter this seemingly closed circle of life and death and get off the reincarnation treadmill? When have we evolved enough for that to happen?

Chapter 13: *Glorious HerStory~The Spontaneous Healing In Overstanding Some Truth of Our Origins

Rewriting a positive end to a story

Truth seeks happy endings. You may not think one has to do with the other but, when you think about it, it makes sense.

We won't get very far if we don't acknowledge and explore the truth—we can't evolve, we can't become enlightened if we don't have the courage to explore what truth is.

And, that truth, in part, is staring up from the Google Earth photographs in the form of Giants who have previously inhabited the planet. They are everywhere, nowhere is there a place where they weren't—we are walking on carcasses right now!

There is nothing in this third dimension that didn't originally come from flesh, blood, and bone. Like I asked at the beginning of this book:

> **We are born with a body only, how does anything else get into this dimension?**

It doesn't—it can't.

This is brought to your attention because I know this to be part of the truth that is being selectively hidden from us. I can't tell you how I know because I don't know how I know. I just do. I'm also very aware that I carry within myself a "Cassandra-like" attribute, where I may be very likely to be right about something but I am not believed or heeded. That's alright—I'm already anticipating just that because I have no credentials.

Or, let's just say I have not been brainwashed by academia away from part of the truth!

They have to know—the elite must know that all worlds, all matter is made from flesh, blood, and bone.

Wars on Earth as well in Heaven—as above, so below. And space smells like steak. Anyone putting this all together?

Study your Google Earth—not on the browser, you need to have the software before they shut that down completely.

Figure 134. (Google, 2017, July 9) Two Giants kissing.

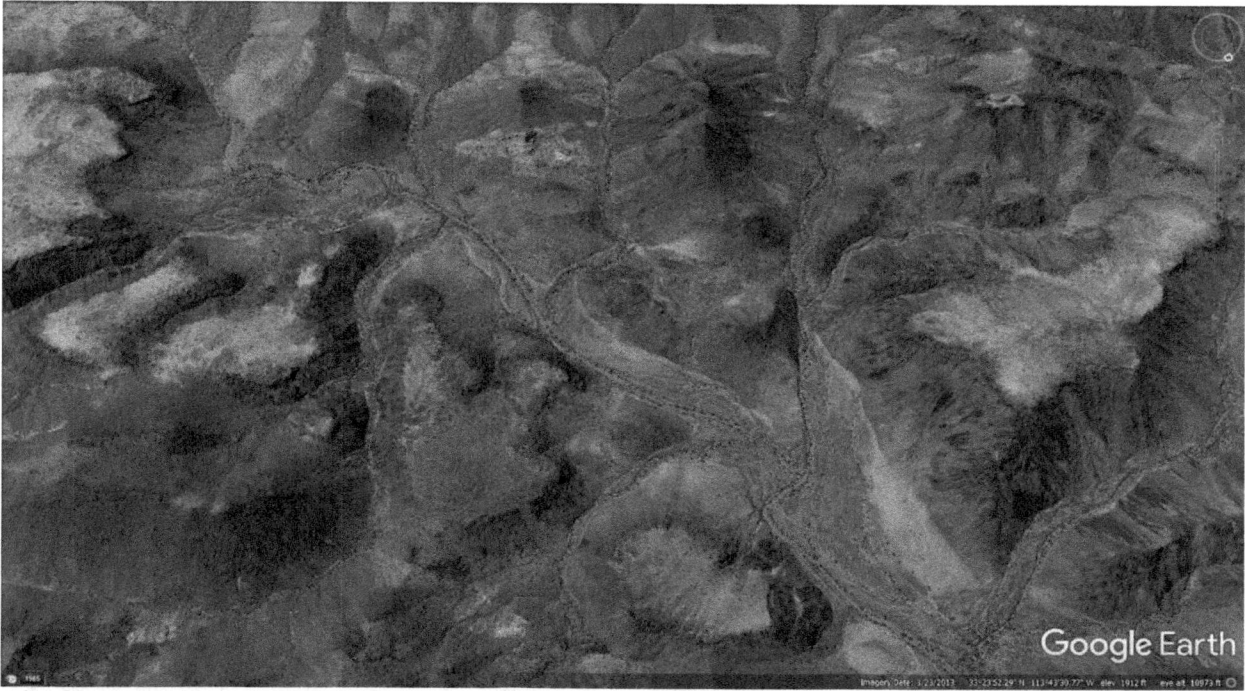

Figure 135. (Google, March 23) Two Giants face to face.

Figure 136. (Google, August 3) Two heads (a hand still holding one) face-to-face.

Figure 137. (Google, 2011, July 15) Two Giants but it could be one big Giants' head split from the top down the middle.

Figure 138. (Google, 2013, December 30) Two Giants holding onto each other—or a Giant's head that's split down the middle.

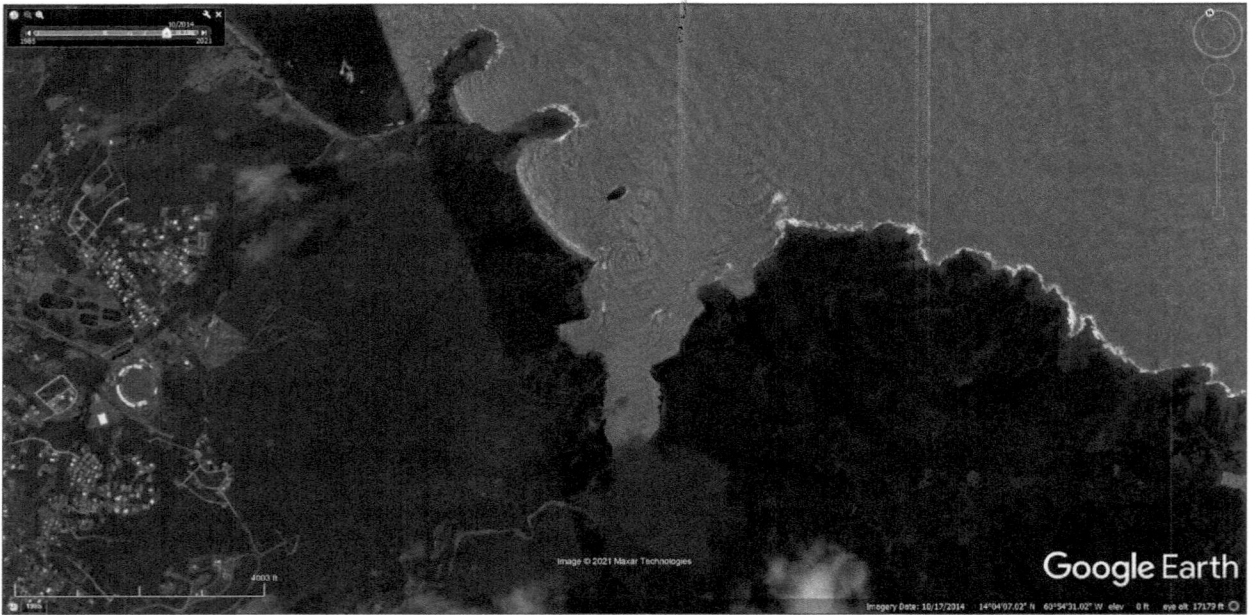

Figure 139. (Google, 2014, October 17) Two Giants, one looks like he has horns.

Look at Zoom Earth. Watch those weather patterns—look at the clouds how they form things...is it pareidolia or could clouds reveal past actions that are heavily written upon the ethers?

The bottom line in all of this is how to reconcile these seeming secrets hiding right in front of our eyes. The idea that the entire planet is made from dead Giants is a difficult pill to swallow. It is paradigm shattering—it'll make one question everything else, especially the deepest questions about our own existence.

And, I hope it does that. Search your soul for the reasons you came to this planet—it's not a one time deal; life. We go around and around, over and over, again and again. Once we have entered the earth's orbit on the soul level, we get "caught" or magnetized to the Earth on a reincarnation treadmill that is difficult to rise above, overcome or ascend beyond.

While we are here on the planet, it's important to maintain a healthy vision for the future. All these doomsday undercurrents are taking its toll on the youth, in America anyways.

And, not just the doomsday stuff but the rising costs of everything: the competition for jobs all while the grade point average in schools goes down and the stress skyrockets from high school on into adulthood. Anxiety and depression are at all time highs, psych drugs are churned out and consumed like they were candy at Halloween.

Dumbing everyone down with GMOs, chemtrails, controlling peoples' actions with direct energy weapons (scalar wave technology), wreaking havoc in the body with preservatives in the food, such as artificial colors and flavors, and processed foods (which is virtually anything frozen); high fructose corn syrup is churning out diabetics everyday in droves.

There is a breakdown of the basic family unit with our high divorce rates, because few are taking their time choosing a proper mate. They get pregnant and you are expected to marry right away; people barely out of their teenage years.

People are herded into apartment dwellings and then stacked up upon each other, which is an unnatural way to live. We were all meant to spread out over the ample lands-each family having enough land under them to grow their own food.

No one can trust the produce they are buying at the supermarket; GMOs dominate the produce industry. Farmers and people growing veggies to sell at the Farmers' Markets may have been cajoled into using GMO seeds for their crops. GMOs are known health hazards (Dona & Arvanitoyannis, 2009).

It gets worse and worse. People in the military come home and are screwed up in some major way. I've seen people come out of the military and quickly become schizophrenic or homeless or addicted. Even if they saw no action, whatever they are being inoculated with seems to sever some vital, internal function that makes it difficult to relate any longer to the mundane world.

What does any of this do with Giants? Nothing directly, because the past is the past. Armageddon has played out already—it's plain to see from some of these photos of Google Earth. We can't let these steady streams of Apocalyptic conditioning be a self-fulfilling prophecy.

We are at the beginning of a brand New Age: The Age of Aquarius which promises to be a more enlightened and truthful state of existence leaving behind the delusive Age of Pisces (where deception and falsehood reigned and has kept us all in the dark ages to this very day).

The Age of Aquarius promises unity, brotherhood and higher altruistic and humanitarian intentions of humankind in general. It also will promote technology but it's imperative to create the correct kind of technology. The kind that helps humankind to evolve rather than merely solve or carry out mundane tasks. But it's already gotten out of hand—just look at the Black Budget that they continue to feed trillions and trillions of valueless dollars into National Security.

We have no enemies that America needs that much weaponry against! It's ridiculous—Star Wars? The sensationalism is a pathetic, mello-dramatic, sweet-16-birthday-party turned temper tantrum all to distract the masses from the underlying issues (like the powers that be running off with big bucks, or what orthodox religion is banning or accepting) which prompted the drama in the first place.

The Catholic Church for example, acknowledging that there may be alien life is suspicious, don't you think? Don't you wonder what the motivation was for the church doing that? If anything, this event is a seeding of sorts into the Catholic peoples' mind-soften the ground so at some point if the powers that be have the military implement false (flag) signs and wonders via Project Blue Beam; people will believe the hologram! Then, there goes even more money into black budget military weaponry and star wars programs. I believe the government would go that far to gather all the resources: gold, metals, gems, oil, water, land, and food they can because, if an apocalypse is coming, it's because they would have caused it.

Ancient prophecy is not prophecy at all! Prophecy is a set of instructions, a guide-to, suggestion(s), both subliminal and right to our faces.

Of course, none of this is directly related to humankind's past alongside Giants. I'm pointing these seemingly unrelated things out because it all fits together—even the lies we have all been taught figure in the plan, obviously.

Everything is built on hierarchies and whenever a hierarchy is implemented, it sets people apart and they become insular to the level they are placed within that hierarchy. The only people to benefit from any hierarchy are the ones who are self-exalted mind you, to occupying the capstone of the hierarchy.

Very little actual ideology is true, through and through. No one school of thought, religion, psychology, new age teaching, philosophy, mystery school, brotherhood is complete and/or 100% truthful.

It's all very simple, it just isn't always easy!

Take the 5% (give or take) of truth that there is in each idea or belief system and build on that and throw the rest out. Everyone who has ever come up with a religion or a philosophy did so out of their own ego base. Hear me out now; it's not so black and white. While I'm positive that it didn't start out this way (one can hope) it certainly ended up being that way because of someone's ego along the way of the ideas development and as the result of other peoples' fixed input and interpretation of dogma specific to the original idea.

Know that your life, my life, everyone's life is a test and a challenge to awaken to our true calling and purpose in life. There is not one person who does not have a rightful and productive place in society from where their talents and gifts can shine and be an inspiration to others. Every person has a purpose specific to where their attention goes and the interests that they have.

Everyone on the planet ought to know what an "inside job" life truly is. If you continue to ignore your pleading insides—telling you this treadmill life from 9 to 5 is bullocks, telling you that many truths are being actively withheld from everyone, that you need to be true to yourself, or you will die without ever knowing, lest fulfilling your true purpose on the planet. You will only have to come back in attempts to remember why you came to this planet and you will keep coming back until you do remember and fulfill your purpose.

Reincarnation itself is a treadmill motion in the astral planes, we are seemingly trapped in this cycle of life, death, regeneration. Lather, rinse and repeat.

I believe the only way to ascend (and to get off the reincarnation treadmill) is to get so "good;" your vibrations surpass being able to hold your consciousness in heavy 3D meat bags such as our bodies are. Get authentically "good" and you will not be able to hold a

3D physical body. Vibrations would be too high. By that time, you will not want or need to incarnate again down into gross fleshly matter.

12 strand DNA activation is what we all should strive for. Reconnecting those bridges from our conscious awareness to multidimensions that we can currently only access out-of-body; awakening those strands will bring out the super-human within each and every one of us.

Autonomy is an important aspect of overall unity within the human race. If we can't be autonomous by ourselves, it'll be twice as hard to do it as a unit if it can be done at all as individuals.

Everyone has an obligation to their fellow man, woman and child; to be truthful and above board. Unassuming and tolerant. To convey their observations about the next guy in a way that is helpful and building up—not scurrilous and tearing one down. Anyone can tear someone else down-that doesn't take intelligence or inner strength.

Intelligence and strength is knowing how to **bridge the gap** so that no one feels alienated and disparate from the tribe. Of course that too takes courage if not perhaps a bit of foolhardiness.

We are our "brother's keepers" in the sense of pulling one's covers-the truth even when it hurts; communicating an honest and straightforward appraisal of how another is doing, how the person's actions affect the rest of the tribe and what can be done to remedy a difficult situation. Firmly but fairly, objectively and without bias.

But in the end we can only save ourselves because it is after all, like I said at the beginning of this book: an inside job.

By giving everyone an equally advantageous way of being able to take care of themselves, we can promote self-sufficiency. We don't enslave others or make others dependent upon us while virtue signaling our actions and then scapegoat the person once they aren't doing something we want or are of no use to us anymore. We don't build someone up just to tear them down so as to build them up again appearing like heroes to the rest of an unwitting world. Stop leveling people against each other. Stop trying to control every action by micromanaging others. Or gross *mis* micromanaging!

Stop being a tyrant and give everyone equal opportunity to advance their lives! What's encouraged for the sons, should be encouraged for the daughters, in the areas of education and self-sufficiency.

Stop measuring the bad antics of others against our self-exalted "good" deeds. Chances are if one is doing that, there was no good intention on one's part to begin with, and one is just looking for a scapegoat.

◆◆◆

I have always been out of step with my own generation. The antipathy is mutual; with 95% of people within 2-3 years older or younger than I, there is a severe disconnect. I simply do not share many of the rigid attitudes towards that most of my peers have and it's alright.

I know why I came to this planet, I know it has absolutely NOTHING to do with accumula—I mean, hoarding money, objects, power or power over the lives of others. I know that we all are supposed to be chasing Peace and Harmony, not some bank.

Having "stuff" isn't going to fill the God-shaped hole in your heart. I know Love is to emanate from the core of our being, to give love and spread joy freely. I know that forgiveness heals hate and disease and is one of the biggest lessons to be learned in sentient consciousness. I know that there is a purpose for everyone—For Everyone. Not one is left not knowing from whence they came and are going.

Practically no one here is truly indigenous to this planet, we are all from various different places all over the cosmos but we all decided to jump into this reincarnation treadmill to further our own soul's journey through Experience and to help others in their soul's journey through Experience. That is after all, the reason for our Soul's journey.

I would say that I'm just as skeptical of mind as I am to run on a blind leap of faith. Depends on what the thing is that I'm looking at.

It's important to look at things from a parallax perspective, simply because things always look different from a particular time in space as well as different vantage points.

No one needs to tell me that the claims I make in this book are outrageous, I know they are because of what I've been taught in school. However I also know that there are myriads of subjects never taught in school that are perfectly valid and true in life. Such as making a budget and balancing a checkbook to cryptozoology. From the mundane to the arcane.

And, like I said at the beginning of this book, read this book objectively and draw your own conclusions. I'm not here to convince anyone who has their mind set against the subject of Giants. Evidence of them is all over Google Earth and it's astounding...

If you study ancient texts like *the Enuma Elish* or *the Book of Giants* (there are many different 'Book of Giants' out there) you'll start to see the fuller picture of Giants as truly being part of our collective history on the planet. I believe Giants to have had more history on this planet than humans of our size anyway.

But, dig deep: this rabbit hole goes such a long and winding way down, around, out, over and through.

I realize this book has been a real mish mash of disjointed, random thoughts. Take what you need from it if anything, and toss the rest.

This whole subject of Giants blindsided me when it crossed my path. For years, I studied Google Earth (Google Sky a lot), for other reasons. I was focused on other things within the program. For years I occasionally saw Giants on Google Earth and filed it away in my memory.

I don't know at what point I began actively searching out what I see as Giants on Google Earth, maybe around 2015-2016. I've been collecting photos of Giants on Google Earth easily into the thousands. Since 2015 I've had probably 6 or 7 computers with hard drives filled with Google Earth photos and videos of various themes in addition to Giants. So I don't have easy access to all I have collected over the years but more than enough to help state my case for this book.

It has been just since around the beginning of the pandemic in March 2020 that I started writing the body of text that is this book—I never imagined I'd write such a thing as this!

It has been a very enlightening, illuminating, paradigm jolting trip and overall once again having to chuck my whole belief system (as is necessary, at times) in a thorough re-vision of what reality really is as well as what it is not.

You are just as far *in* as you are *out*.

Figure 140. (Google, 2019, September 26) Giant carrying another Giant.

Figure 141. (Google, 2016, March 1) Giant carrying another Giant.

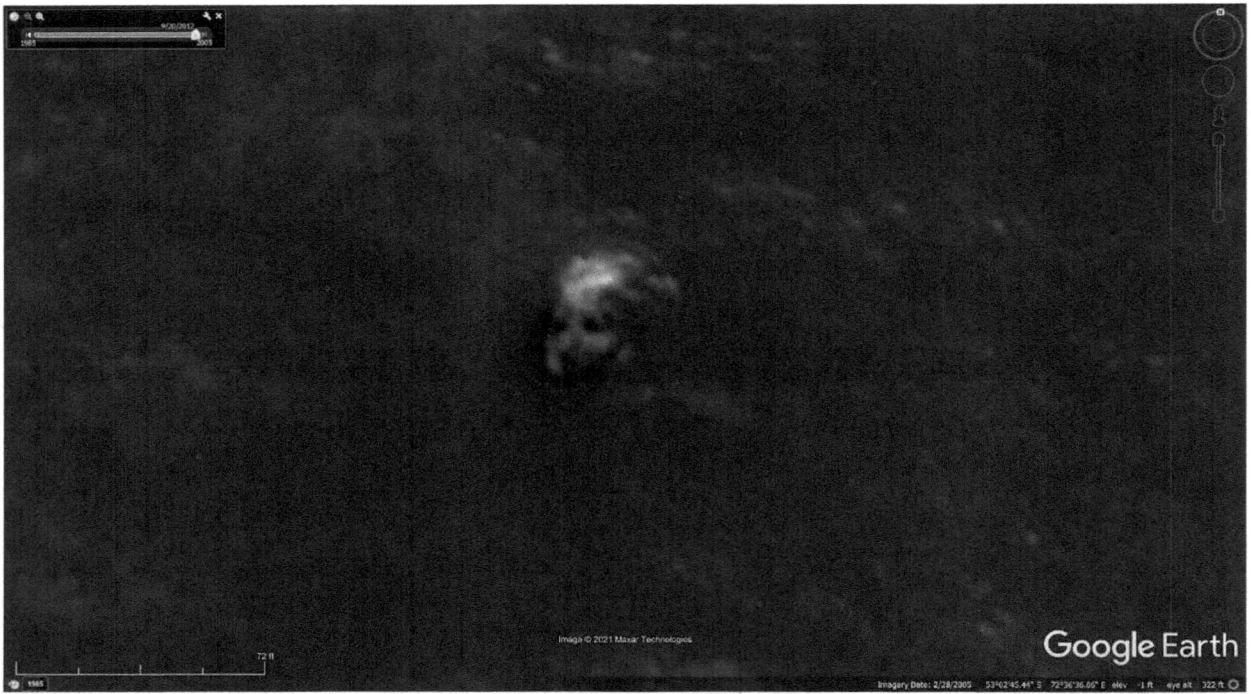

Figure 142. (Google, 2005, February 28). Giant's head in the water.

References

Arraf, J. (2021). *Iraq reclaims 17,000 looted artifacts, its biggest-ever repatriation.* The New York Times. nytimes.com/2021/08/03/world/middleeast/iraq-looted-artifacts-return.html

Dona, A & Arvanitoyannis, I. (2009). Health risks of genetically modified foods. *Critical reviews in food science and nutrition* 49(2), 164-175.

Kósa, G. (2018). The Book of Giants tradition in the Chinese Manichaica. In *Ancient tales of giants from Qumran and Turfan: Proceedings of an international conference at Munich, Germany (June 6-8, 2014)* (eds. Stuckenbruck & Morano). Mohr Siebek.

Ritschel, C. (2020). *'Gunpowder, seared steak, raspberries and rum': New fragrance recreates the smell of space.* Independent.co.uk. independent.co.uk/tech/space-fragrance-perfume-nasa-scent-astronauts-kickstarter-a9598406.html.

List of Figures

25. Google (2001, December 30). [62°07'57.26"S, 63°06'31.13"W]. earth.google.com.

26. Google (2005, December 11). [49°39'55.11"S, 178°46'34.64"E]. earth.google.com.

27. Google (2007, March 30). [4°00'51.83"N, 81°36'15.83"W]. earth.google.com.

28. Zoom (n.d.). [22°12'N, 149°24"W]. zoom.earth.

29. Zoom (n.d.). [68°54'S, 107°54'E]. zoom.earth.

30. Zoom (n.d.). [53°24'S, 106°06'W]. zoom.earth.

31. Zoom (n.d.). [53°42'N, 95°06'W]. zoom.earth.

32. Zoom (n.d.). [45°42'N, 68°24'E]. zoom.earth.

33. Zoom (n.d.). [35°06'N, 161°30'W]. zoom.earth.

34. Zoom (n.d.). [13°46'37"N, 131°24'50'W]. zoom.earth.

35. Google (2021). [5°26'47.38"S, 53°19'39.76"E]. earth.google.com.

36. Google (1998). [63°19'29.98"S, 58°42'13.54"W]. earth.google.com.

37. Google (2015). [18°20'53.84"S, 162°08'12.18"W]. earth.google.com.

38. Google (2012). [72°07'05.54"S, 169°24'03.43"W]. earth.google.com.

39. Google (n.d.). [79°57'03.49"N, 50°14'05.69"E]. earth.google.com.

40. Google (2011, December 30). [73°24'37.55"S, 22°23'49.75"W]. earth.google.com.

41. Google (2010, January 3). [72°33'39.41"S, 170°00'29.71"E]. earth.google.com.

42. Google (2016, December 30). [67°32'34.04"S, 68°09'42.25"E]. earth.google.com.

43. Google (2017, January 5). [57°05'04.2"S, 26°44'54.18"W]. earth.google.com.

44. Google (2012, October 7). [72°21'02.34"S, 169°51'49.52"E]. earth.google.com.

45. Google (n.d.). [72°22'4.08"S, 169°53'38.63"E]. earth.google.com.

46. Google (2017, July 23). [53°04'49.15"S, 73°29'20.58"E]. earth.google.com.

47. Google (2009, February 3). [53°07'36.80"S, 73°34'38.25"E]. earth.google.com.

48. Google (2016, December 30). [70°05'34.98"S, 5°46'03.38"E]. earth.google.com.

49. Google (2015, October 29). [53°07'22.03"S, 73°32'48.64"E]. earth.google.com.

50. Google (n.d.). [80°01'20.82"N, 51°14'10.58"E]. earth.google.com.

51. Google (2012, January 17). [70°38'50.26"S, 68°41'28.90"E]. earth.google.com.

52. Google (2010, December 9). [59°28'49.22"S, 27°12'50.08"W]. earth.google.com.

53. Google (n.d.). [59°26'48.39"S, 27°14'41.16"W]. earth.google.com.

54. Google (2014, February 5). [53°07'04.00"S, 73°34'48.63"E]. earth.google.com.

55. Google (2012, October 27). [71°35'53.96"S, 170°24'52.93"E]. earth.google.com.

56. Google (2012, October 27). [71°35'54.75"S, 170°24'39.30"E]. earth.google.com.

57. Google (2014, February 5). [53°06'15'25"S, 73°33'23.94"E]. earth.google.com.

58. Google (2022). [53°06'20.75"S, 73°31'05.75"E]. earth.google.com.

59. Google (2009, February 3). [53°07'31.20"S, 73°34'32.99"E]. earth.google.com.

60. Google (2003, December 30). [73°03'35.66"S, 109°07'38.31"W]. earth.google.com.

61. Google (2009, February 3). [53°07'04.61"S, 73°34'15.93"E]. earth.google.com.

62. Google (2009, February 3). [53°07'24.85"S, 73°34'07.54"E]. earth.google.com.

63. Google (n.d.). [13°55'34.84"S, 170°45'51.37"W]. earth.google.com.

64. Google (2015, December 30). [14°50'05.55"S, 167°18'45.76"W]. earth.google.com.

65. Google (2015, December 13). [3°14'34.56"N, 166°06'32.13"E]. earth.google.com.

66. Google (n.d.). [20°21'08.71"S, 155°44'43.45"E]. earth.google.com.

67. Google (n.d.). [11°16'49.31"N, 123°45'29.80"E]. earth.google.com.

68. Google (2014, April 5). [35°49'21.73"E, 35°49'21.73"E]. earth.google.com.

69. Google (2009, February 3). [53°07'09.37"S, 73°32'58.58"E]. earth.google.com.

70. Google (2001). [30°42'58.58"N, 78°43'53.85"E]. earth.google.com.

71. Google (2019, March 29). [46°24'07.92"S, 51°40'58.86"E]. earth.google.com.
72. Google (2012, June 22). [12°12'35.03"S, 96°53'07.20"E]. earth.google.com.
73. Google (n.d.). [9°54'20.23"N, 76°05'22.63"W]. earth.google.com.
74. Google (n.d.). [40°53'04.22"N, 75°57'21.13"W]. earth.google.com.
75. Google (n.d.). [50°01'30.72"N, 119°56'57.73"W]. earth.google.com.
76. Google (n.d.). [47°33'04.54"N, 102° 23'01.18"W]. earth.google.com.
77. Google (n.d.). [39°43'37.53'N, 94°29'27.66"W]. earth.google.com.
78. Google (n.d.). [19°14'04.20"S, 110°53'22.04"E]. earth.google.com.
79. Google (n.d.). [26°12'07.76"S, 118°23'05.87"E]. earth.google.com.
80. Google (n.d.). [64°46'33.35"N, 6°37'48.73"W]. earth.google.com.
81. Google (2009, February 3). [53°05'54.94"S, 73°30'35.14"E]. earth.google.com.
82. Google (2013, December 27). [46°23'58.72"S, 51°41'19.87"E]. earth.google.com.
83. Google (2020, July 27). [74°25'34.09"N, 18°56'28.05"E]. earth.google.com.
84. Google (2017, November 1). [54°39'39.19"S, 158°50'35.31"E]. earth.google.com.
85. Google (2019, September 11). [37°23'57.69"N, 108°01'25.13"W]. earth.google.com.
86. Google (2021). [74°23'11.70"N, 18°56'37.39"E]. earth.google.com.
87. Google (2005, August 16). [5°53'04.35"S, 53°01'35.37"E]. earth.google.com.
88. Google (2022). [54°04'59.13"S, 37°02'40.44"W]. earth.google.com.
89. Google (2013, August 3). [45°02'22.25"N, 108°40'13.54"W]. earth.google.com.
90. Google (2013, May 9). [31°31'39.81"N, 114°03'01.48"W]. earth.google.com.
91. Google (2020, July 27). [74°24'40.62"N, 18°58'13.66"E]. earth.google.com.
92. Google (2009, January 31). [34°15'14.29"N, 116°22'40.63"W]. earth.google.com.
93. Google (n.d.). [66°01'44.16"S, 50°40'11.59"E]. earth.google.com.
94. Google (n.d.). [65°57'21.33"S, 49°58'16.39"E]. earth.google.com.
95. Google (2013, December 30). [30°54'19.31"N, 82°11'12.63"E]. earth.google.com.
96. Google (2020, July 27). [74°26'28.89"N, 19°13'13.45"E]. earth.google.com.
97. Google (1996, December 30). [63°38'52.85"N, 17°59'40.16"W]. earth.google.com.
98. Google (2012, December 30). [75°100'36.33"N, 143°03'07.24"E]. earth.google.com.
99. Google (2012, December 30). [74°52'42.06"N, 142°23'12.61"E]. earth.google.com.
100.   Google (n.d.). [7°26'2.86"W, 64°29'22.70"N]. earth.google.com.
101.   Google (2015, January 4). [22°20'17.73"S, 40°22'14.31"E]. earth.google.com.
102.   Google (2020, July 27). [74°23'26.01"N, 18°56'52.62"E]. earth.google.com.
103.   Google (2016, December 30). [69°52'06.83"S, 9°03'45.97"E]. earth.google.com.
104.   Google (2015. September 30). [46°56'54.31"E, 37°56'54.31"E]. earth.google.com.
105.   Google (2015, September 30). [46°38'09.05"S, 37°56'18.53"E]. earth.google.com.
106.   Google (2019, September 8). [30°45'49.06"N, 79°25'43.67"E]. earth.google.com.
107.   Google (2013, December 30). [54°28'54.20"S, 3°31'22.65"E]. earth.google.com.
108.   Google (2021). [31°36'30.16"N, 113°50'35.81"W]. earth.google.com.
109.   Google (2019, June 24). [28°24'07.65"N, 59°37'12.61"E]. earth.google.com.
110.   Google (2008, December 30). [78°11'06.49"S, 165°20'30.76"E]. earth.google.com.
111.   Google (2006, February 27). [67°38'02.80"S, 68°24'15.11"W]. earth.google.com.
112.   Google (2008, January 14). [37°51'13.66"S, 77°31'16.06"E]. earth.google.com.
113.   Google (2014, October 7). [15°09'51.91"S, 40°34'12.40"E]. earth.google.com.

114.   Google (2016, December 30). [10°12'11.92"S, 32°51'06.91"E]. earth.google.com.

115.   Google (2018, December 14). [30°14'34.76"N, 79°o6'50.46"E]. earth.google.com.

116.   Google (2015, December 13). [34°40'05.38"N, 119°44'12.33"E]. earth.google.com.

117.   Google (2019, September 8). [30°44'54.93"N, 79°24'34.21"E]. earth.google.com.

118.   Google (2022). [46°25'43.84"S, 52°16'38.37"E]. earth.google.com.

119.   Google (2011). [46°06'24.40"S, 50°11'44.59"E]. earth.google.com.

120.   Google (2021). [30°43'43.89"N, 78°44'28.26"E]. earth.google.com.

121.   Google (2016, March 1). [46°37'11.51"S, 37°55'17.30"E]. earth.google.com.

122.   Google (2006, February 13). [46°23'19.38"S, 51°44'57.22"E]. earth.google.com.

123.   Google (2016, February 24). [46°49'12.03"S, 37°43'41.25"E]. earth.google.com.

124.   Google (2008, September 5). [9°38'24.29"S, 32°07'51.74"E]. earth.google.com.

125.   Google (2020, September 24). [7°50'49.00"N, 123°33'15.87"E]. earth.google.com.

126.   Google (n.d.). [79°41'31.17"N, 3°16'16.58"E]. earth.google.com.

127.   Google (2020, October 8). [33°16'36.34"N, 76°26'15.55"E]. earth.google.com.

128.   Google (2016, December 30). [45°24'25.91"N, 85°58'43.44"E]. earth.google.com.

129.   Google (2011, August 9). [71°01'43.35"N, 7°59'03.82"W]. earth.google.com.

130.   Google (2011, December 30). [50°45'13.88"N, 82°45'20.26"E]. earth.google.com.

131.   Google (2014, December 30). [66°39'29.00"S, 70°14'01.63"W]. earth.google.com.

132.   Google (2000, December 30). [73°09'02.92"S, 83°26'50.01"W]. earth.google.com.

133.   Google (2019, March 29). [46°22'18.44"S, 51°38'52.61"E]. earth.google.com.

134.   Google (2014, July 9). [74°22'39.90"N, 18°58.47.10"E]. earth.google.com.

135.   Google (2013, March 23). [33°23'52.29"N, 113°43'30.77"W]. earth.google.com.

136.   Google (2013, August 3). [45°11'12.87"N, 108°43'05.38"W]. earth.google.com.

137.   Google (2011, July 15). [11°28'51.87"S, 33°18'56.64"E]. earth.google.com.

138.   Google (2013, December 30). [71°27'14.44"S, 97°05'16.79"W]. google.earth.com.

139.   Google (2014, October 17). [14°04'07.02"N, 60°54'31.02"W]. earth.google.com.

140.   Google (2019, September 28). [1°06'56.02"S, 37°45'13.82"E]. earth.google.com.

141.   Google (2016, March 1). [46°39'39.78"S, 37°57'43.45"E]. earth.google.com.

142.   Google (2005, February 28). [53°02'45.44"S, 72°36'36.06"E]. earth.google.com.

www.ingramcontent.com/pod-product-compliance
Lightning Source LLC
Chambersburg PA
CBHW081418090426
42738CB00017B/3403